THE
GOLF
HANDBOOK

THE
GOLF
HANDBOOK

THE COMPLETE GUIDE TO THE GREATEST GAME

VIVIEN SAUNDERS

INTRODUCED BY

PETER ALLISS

PAN BOOKS LTD
London, Sydney and Auckland

A Marshall Edition
Conceived, edited and designed by
Marshall Editions Ltd
170 Piccadilly
London W1V 9DD

First published in Great Britain 1989 by Pan Books Ltd
Cavaye Place, London SW10 9PG

9 8 7 6 5

ISBN 0 330 30762 2

Copyright © 1989 by Marshall Editions Ltd

Managing Editor: Ruth Binney
Editor: Julian Worthington
Art Director: Dave Allen
Design Assistant: Jonathan Bigg
Picture Editor: Zilda Tandy
Production: Barry Baker
                   Janice Storr

Illustrated by Mike Bilsland

Typeset by MS Filmsetting Ltd, Frome, UK
Origination by Regent Publishing Services Ltd,
Hong Kong
Printed in Italy

CONTENTS

THE GREATEST GAME

I do hope there's going to be room out there for all the new players our game is attracting. There's hardly a taxi-driver in London who's not seeking a hint or two whenever I step into his cab. In France, the game is *le plus chic*, and I hear complaints in Spain that Scandinavian visitors have the unfair advantage of the midnight sun to practise by.

Golf is blossoming the world over, producing teenage caddies in Queensland who, it turns out as they advise you on your fourth shot from the bunker, play off scratch, to Floridians whose daily and not unrealistic ambition is to go round in one under their age.

And who would have expected that golf would establish itself as a television treat? Just as a matter of logistics, if a snooker table fills the screen and a football pitch requires the views of a dozen cameras, how do they manage to cover the action over a hundred or so acres?

Mostly, perhaps, the appeal of the game lies in the splendidly calm sportsmanship of golfers. Not for them screaming at umpires or kissy celebrations. A discreet hop and a skip when the thirty footer drops, maybe, but otherwise no more than a wry smile or a shake of the head to tell you how they're feeling. On view is the deep, contemplative attack of players who have only themselves to beat, no one else to blame, cocooned in concentration, respectful of the others sharing the arena.

Golf at the highest levels is one of the loneliest of games. And yet we can imagine ourselves as one of those sunlit stars much more readily than a tennis tyro can imagine holding up an end at Wimbledon. "I've parred that very hole," we say. Or "I hit an eight iron just like that only last Saturday."

Vivien Saunders understands those samenesses. And the differences. She was the first European lady to qualify for the US tour and British Ladies Open Champion in 1977. She is now introducing beginners to the game, as well as keeping an eye on the national teams of several countries. They used to say he who can does; he who cannot, teaches. Vivien can, and does, and teaches.

With this book's demonstration of her explanatory skills, I shall have a quick suggestion for the next cab-driver who takes his hands off the wheel to get my opinion of his grip. But as for where he can practise, that's a long game.

INTRODUCTION

Whether you are a beginner or a scratch player – or even a non-golfer just
enthralled by watching the game – *The Golf Handbook* has something for
everyone.

Obviously the ideal way to learn to play or, equally, to iron out those niggling
faults that are holding back your handicap, is out on the course with a
professional. But there is much you can do yourself – at home, in the back
garden or playing by yourself or with friends. *The Golf Handbook* has been
specifically designed as a self-help guide to every aspect of technique.
Depending on your own ability, you may feel you need to start again from the
beginning. By working your way through from the very basics of play and
practising as outlined in each section of the book you should soon see a
marked improvement.

By breaking down technique into individual categories and looking at specific
problems on the course the value of *The Golf Handbook* to low handicap
players is assured. They can use it to analyse those aspects of play that need
rethinking or improving, without necessarily changing their style or technique
completely.

Of course it is not possible to carry your copy with you when you are out
playing a round. For this reason I have included basic hints to remember,
which highlight the key points of individual techniques and situations that you
are likely to face. For while you need to work hard to correct or improve your
technique, you should never get bogged down with detail during a game. The
most important point to remember is: keep it simple. And that applies as much
to your mental approach as any specific aspect of your play.

But *The Golf Handbook* is not just about technique. There are also important
sections on practice and how to improve your play tactically. There are also
hints on keeping fit, a vital element for any serious golfer. And there is general
information on equipment and clothing to help you sort out exactly what you
need from the vast selection available.

To complete your enjoyment of the book – and the game itself – I have also
included a brief history of golf, how and where it is played and some of the
great names of the past and present we all strive to emulate.

Like all sports, golf is above all a game to be enjoyed and I hope that you will
get as much fun reading and learning from *The Golf Handbook* as I have had
writing it.

Vivien Saunders

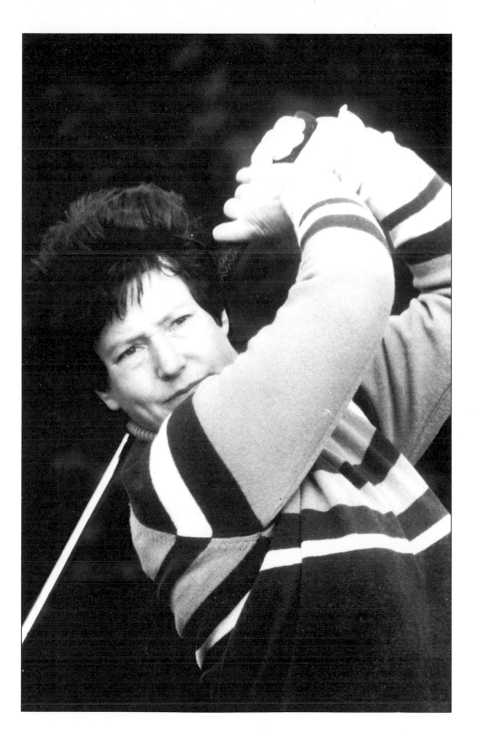

THE GAME OF GOLF: 1

No one knows the precise origins of the game of golf. Some suggest it really began in medieval times, with shepherds hitting pebbles around the hillsides with their crooks to while away the hours spent tending the sheep.

Another suggestion is that the game derived from the ancient Flemish pastime of chole, which was already known about and played in England by the mid 14th century.

Perhaps the most likely forerunner was the Dutch game of *kolf*, documented as early as the end of the 13th century and portrayed in many Dutch landscape paintings by the 16th century. "Golfers" certainly played cross-country with a stick and ball, not into a hole but to certain landmarks, usually doors on specific buildings.

It was in Scotland, however, that the game really developed. Up and down the east coast it apparently became so popular a pastime that in 1457 James II, in an Act of Parliament, banned golf – and football too – because they were interfering with archery practice. Skill with the bow and arrow was crucial to keeping the English out of Scotland.

The game remained uniquely Scottish – perhaps with its Dutch counterpart of *kolf* – until James VI of Scotland also became King of England and took the game south with him. At Blackheath, now Royal Blackheath in South London, the Scottish noblemen laid out a seven-hole course to enable them to continue playing their beloved game.

When the Scottish noblemen came south with their king – James VI – to London, one priority was to provide facilities for their beloved game of golf **(below)**. So they had a course built at Blackheath on the outskirts of the city.

Golf was traditionally the sport of noblemen, although later golf societies were set up for the artisan as well. Today people from all walks of life play the game – including film stars. Here Clint Eastwood **(right)** is getting some useful tips on how he should hold the club from Australian Greg Norman during the AT & T National Pro-am tournament.

THE GAME OF GOLF: 2

Golf caddies at the turn of this century – a far cry from those seen on today's courses. Their function was quite different, too. Apart from the fact that golfers used far fewer clubs, the caddies had to clear the way ahead and also watch out for the flying balls.

12

The early courses in Scotland bore little resemblance to those of today. The game was played over public land – as in places it still is – with natural hazards and obstacles to negotiate. Not only were walls and ditches part of the game, but players often had to thread their way through others out enjoying their various recreations – horse racing, cricket, picnicking and so on.

Caddies were hired by the golfers, not just to carry the clubs – golf bags were not invented until around 1870 – but to help make a way through the other activities on the links and presumably to watch out for the ball.

Courses were natural, manicured only by sheep and rabbits. There were no formal tees as such; players simply teed up a few feet from the previous hole.

Rules, of course, developed over the years and golf clubs were formed. The oldest of these, the Honourable Company of Edinburgh Golfers – now based at Muirfield – was founded in 1744, while ten years later the Society of St Andrews' Golfers was created.

The rules of the various clubs and courses were standardized, following St Andrews' lead in using 18 holes. Before 1764 the course at St Andrews had comprised 22 holes, others as few as six and as many as 25. But by 1858 it had

been agreed. The Society of St Andrews' Golfers, having become the Royal and Ancient Golf Club of St Andrews in 1834, now ruled that the round of golf should be 18 holes. And so it has remained.

The game developed rapidly and began to be played professionally in the mid 1800s. Allan Robertson, the first great professional golfer, died in 1858. Some say that his death prompted the first professional championship at Prestwick in 1860 to find a new national champion.

In 1987 Ian Woosnam's prize money totalled £1,042,622. He was subsequently voted Golfer of the Year.

The Morrises – Tom Morris Snr and Young Tom Morris – were members of the most famous golfing family in the Game. Between them they won the "British Open" no less than eight times.

This competition was opened to amateurs in 1861 to become the first Open Championship. In 1863 it attracted prize money for the winner of just £10. In 1861 it was won by Tom Morris Snr ("Old Tom Morris"), who was successful on three further occasions.

In 1868 the Open was won by his teenage son "Young Tom Morris", who succeeded in winning it three times in a row. Under the rules, he kept the existing trophy, then had to wait for a year while the Open was suspended, pending the creation of a new trophy – the coveted jug. He proceeded to win that too, making it a record four Opens in a row.

From there the game developed to the one we know today. But looking back to when Tom Morris won £10 for the first Open Championship, few would have thought that golfers would one day become millionaires overnight. In 1987 Ian Woosnam achieved just that, winning a $1 million tournament in South Africa.

GOLFING GREATS: 1

Over the last 100 or so years of major championship golf, there have been many great players from all around the world who would arguably be included in many enthusiasts' hall of fame. Comparisons are all too often odious, since individual performances and achievements have to be taken in context – of the time, the conditions, the standard of competition and so on. Included here are those most likely to be selected by a majority of golfers.

Harry Vardon (1870–1937)
Born in Jersey, Harry Vardon won a record six British Opens and one US Open. He popularized, though did not invent, the Vardon grip and undoubtedly revolutionized the game through the unprecedented power of his play. With J. H. Taylor and James Braid – the Great Triumvirate – he dominated the game for almost 25 years. At the age of 50, he was still good enough to be runner-up in the US Open.

Walter Hagen (1892–1969)
Born in Rochester, New York, Hagen won 11 major championships – two US Opens, four British Opens and five USPGA Championships, including four in a row from 1924 to 1927. He captained the first six American Ryder Cup teams. His catchphrase at any tournament was "Who's going to be second?" Hagen travelled around the world giving exhibition matches and living an exciting lifestyle. If not a millionaire, he certainly lived like one.

Robert Tyre (Bobby) Jones Jnr (1902–1971)
Bobby Jones played all his golf as an amateur. A lawyer and engineering graduate, he won five US Amateur Championships, four US Opens, three British Opens and one British Amateur, all in the space of eight years – and before the age of 30. In 1930 he won the Grand Slam – the Open and Amateur Championships of America and Britain – and then retired from competitive golf to concentrate on his profession and to devote time to his family.

Following his retirement, Jones joined forces with Clifford Roberts, a banker, to establish the Augusta National Golf Club and with it the Masters Championship. The course at Augusta, designed by Alister Mackenzie, was opened and hosted the first US Masters in 1934. Each year an invited field of amateurs and professionals competes for the coveted green jacket for the winner. Prize money, though substantial, is never mentioned.

Jones was one of the great writers about the game. His books and articles were highly perceptive.

Henry Cotton (1907–1988)
Born in Cheshire, Henry Cotton won three Open Championships between 1934 and 1948. Had World War II not intervened, he would no doubt have won more. He wrote widely on golf, was involved in course

Harry Vardon, best known for his grip.

Walter Hagen, who lived like a millionaire and always expected to come first.

design and even put on an act at the London Palladium. He played in three Ryder Cup matches and captained the British team twice. He was largely responsible for the increased stature of the golf professional, demanding higher fees and better conditions and obtaining acceptance for professionals in golf clubs. He moved to Portugal on his retirement, designing the course at Penina, and teaching actively until shortly before his death.

Byron Nelson (1912–   )
Byron Nelson won two Masters Championships, two USPGA Championships and the US Open. But what he is best remembered for by his fellow tournament professionals are two remarkable golf seasons. In 1944 he played in 23 professional tournaments and won 13 of them. Opinion was that

Henry Cotton, the first "professional".

GOLFING GREATS: 2

this would never be equalled. In 1945 he improved on this, winning 18 of the 30 US Tour events and coming second in seven others. His stroke average of 68.33 remains unbeaten. Two years later he retired from competitive play, to teach golf and commentate on television.

Ben Hogan (1912–)
Born in Texas, Hogan is legendary for his technique and dedication to practice. Having won two USPGA Championships and the US Open between 1946 and 1948, he suffered an horrific car crash in 1949, after which doctors thought he would never walk again, let alone play golf. But the following year he won the US Open again and in 1953 won the three major championships he played in – the British Open, the US Masters and the US Open. The Grand Slam was impossible – in that year the USPGA Championship clashed with the British Open!

Sam Snead (1912–)
"Slamming Sam" Snead is renowned for his classic swing and the ability to go on playing top-class golf at a reasonably advanced age. The winner of three USPGA Championships, three Masters and the British Open, and eight Ryder Cup appearances with three as captain, Sam Snead has recorded 84 US Tour tournament victories. He was the first to beat 60 for a round and the first to beat his age on the tour – 66 at the age of 67.

Bobby Locke (1917–1987)
Born in South Africa, and considered by many to have been the best putter the game has ever known, Bobby Locke looked the most unlikely of champions. Not only did his baggy plus-fours betray his athleticism, but every shot he hit, including the putts, had alarming spin and curve on them from right to left. Locke won four British Opens from 1949 to 1957. His first visit to America in 1947 produced six wins in the 12 tournaments he entered, putting him second in the money-earning list for the year. But he

preferred Britain and South Africa, playing every day although supposedly very rarely practising.

Peter Thomson (1929–)
Like Bobby Jones, Peter Thomson is a man of many talents and interests. Born in Melbourne, he is also a writer and course architect, with wide interests that include politics and music. Thomson won five British Opens – three in a row from 1954 to 1956, then again in 1958 and 1965. At one time the Americans doubted his ability because of his choice not to compete in America. But with the advent of the Senior Tour in the USA, Thomson has again proved just what an exceptional player he is.

Arnold Palmer (1929–)
American Arnold Palmer has probably done more to make golf a major spectator sport than anyone else. He has the charisma of a movie star and a golf game loved by the public. He hit sensational shots, followed by the odd one that clattered into the trees. His recovery shots were spectacular. Golf became a television sport and with it big money was on offer. Palmer won seven major championships from 1960 to 1964, was in six winning World Cup teams and the individual winner in 1967. In effect, he turned a minority sport into a major one.

Billy Casper (1931–)
Born in California, Billy Casper is the master putter. A member of eight US Ryder Cup teams and winner on five occasions of the coveted Vardon Trophy for the lowest scoring average on the USPGA Tour. Twice he was America's leading money winner.

Michael Bonallack (1934–)
Perhaps the last great amateur in top-class golf, Essex-born Michael Bonallack won five British Amateur Championships, eight English Matchplay and Strokeplay

Arnold Palmer, the charismatic champion.

GOLFING GREATS: 3

18

Championships and played in nine Walker Cup teams against the USA amateurs. His last appearance was in 1971 as captain when the team was victorious at St Andrews. Bonallack's swing was far from orthodox, the clubshaft often bouncing on his left shoulder at the top of the backswing. But what he lost through the green he made up for with demon putting and an exceptional temperament. In 1984 he was appointed secretary of the Royal and Ancient at St Andrews.

Gary Player (1935–   )
At 5 feet 7 inches, Gary Player seemed an unlikely candidate as the third member of golf's Big Three with Nicklaus and Palmer. But the diminutive South African made up for his physical size with a punishing schedule of fitness training and a dedication to practice quite unequalled in professional golf. Player also had willpower and a belief both in God and himself which carried him through tournament after tournament. With more

than 120 major victories to his name, including all the four majors and five World Matchplay Championships, Player is now a major force on the lucrative US Senior Tour.

Jack Nicklaus (1940–   )
Jack Nicklaus is unquestionably the finest golfer of all time. Born in Columbus, Ohio, he has in his memorable career on the course won 20 major championships – his first the US Amateur as a teenager of 19 and the last to date the 1986 US Masters at the age of 46.

Lee Trevino (1940–   )
The wise-cracking Texas-born Mexican with the self-taught swing, Lee Trevino learnt the pressures of the game as a hustler at a public course. Trevino was about to quit the US Tour in 1967, when his wife pawned their belongings to pay for his entry to the US Open. He finished fifth, went on to win it the next year and has never looked back since.

19

Gary Player (above left) – small in stature but a golfing giant on the world's championship courses.

Jack Nicklaus (above) was initially unpopular with the fans for deposing America's favourite sportsman, Arnold Palmer, from his throne. But his magnificent style of golf soon won them over.

Lee Trevino (right), one of the game's most popular and entertaining champions, epitomizes the "rags to riches" fairytale come true.

GOLFING GREATS: 4

Tony Jacklin (1944–   )
Born in Scunthorpe, Lincolnshire, Tony
Jacklin played his way into the record
books by winning the 1969 British Open
(the first Briton to do so for 18 years) and
then the 1970 US Open – the first British
winner for 50 years. He is a perennial
favourite at home and currently captain of
the triumphant Ryder Cup team that has
restored the fortunes of European golf.

Tom Watson (1949–   )
When Tom Watson emerged on the US
Tour, the press doubted his ability to win.
The Kansas City golfer would get into a
winning position and then choke.

   But Tom, a psychology graduate from
Stanford, soon confounded his critics and
became the most consistent golfer in the
world, winning five British Opens from
1975 to 1983, as well as the US Open and
US Masters. In 1977 he won the British
Open in a classic head-to-head contest
against Jack Nicklaus. Never ahead until
the last two holes, Watson completed the
final 36 holes in 65 and 65 to Nicklaus's
65 and 66. In 1982, he snatched victory
from Jack again in the US Open at Pebble
Beach with a spectacular chip at the 71st
hole.

Greg Norman (1955–   )
Golf's "great white shark", the jet-setting
Australian started the game as a caddie
for his mother. Having lost in a play-off
for the US Open title in 1984, Norman
became leading money winner in America
in 1986 and won the British Open the
same year.

Seve Ballesteros (1957–   )
The dashing Spaniard with the charisma
and crowd appeal of Arnold Palmer, Seve
has been the most exciting golfer of the
seventies and eighties. The youngest of
four brothers, all professional golfers,
Seve learnt the game as a caddie, playing
around with odd clubs, manufacturing all
manner of shots and developing an
unrivalled touch around the greens.

Tony Jacklin (left)
achieved the Open
"double" in 1969/70 and
now leads the successful
European Ryder Cup
team.

Greg Norman (right):
this Australian rates as
one of the game's longest
hitters.

**Tom Watson (below
left)** dominated the world
scene for nearly a
decade, due largely to his
consistency.

**Seve Ballesteros
(below):** the golfing flair
of this Spaniard led to a
meteoric rise to fame.

21

GOLFING GREATS: 5

Nick Faldo is England's hero of the late 1980s.

Nick Faldo (1957–   )

Winning the 1989 Masters gave the tall (6ft 3in) Englishman his second Grand Slam victory, to add to the British Open title of 1987. A third just eluded him when he lost the play-off for the US Open in 1988. On the European circuit alone he has won more than £1,000,000 and he has been in the Ryder Cup team since 1979.

Sandy Lyle (1958–   )

The amiable Scot who has done much to put the pride back into British golf with memorable victories in the 1985 British Open and the 1988 US Masters.

Joyce Wethered (1901–   )

Four times British Ladies Amateur champion, Joyce Wethered (Lady Heathcote Amery) was heralded by Bobby Jones as the finest golfer – man or woman – he had ever seen.

Babe Zaharias (1914–1956)

Having won two gold medals in athletics at the 1932 Olympics, "The Babe" turned to golf. Her enormously long hitting brought her several important victories – the US Amateur, the US Open and the British Amateur Championships. One of golf's real entertainers.

Mickey Wright (1935–   )

Born in San Diego, Mickey Wright was probably the greatest woman golfer of all time. She won four US Opens and was six-times winner of the Vare Trophy for the lowest scoring average, four-times leading money winner, with 82 tournament victories in all on the US Tour. In 1961 she won 10 tournaments – and 13 in 1963. Her fear of flying meant that she rarely travelled outside America and her retiring nature perhaps brought her less recognition than she deserved.

Kathy Whitworth (1939–   )

Texas-born, Kathy Whitworth has won more tournaments on the USLPGA Tour than any other player, but never the US Open.

Joe Anne Carner (1939–   )

Born in Massachusetts, Jo Anne Carner was five times US Amateur Champion between 1957 and 1968, before turning professional at the age of 30. She twice won the US Open and has been the outstanding player on the USLPGA Tour.

Sandy Lyle – a champion Scot.

Nancy Lopez (1957–   )

The real star of the USLPGA Tour since 1978, Nancy Lopez emerged that year as a newcomer in her first full pro season to win nine tournaments, including five in a row. A devoted wife and mother as well as a glamorous golfer, Nancy has brought a new popularity to women's professional golf and turned it into a major television sport in America.

Babe Zaharias (left), the athlete turned champion golfer. **Kathy Whitworth (above),** a prolific tournament winner. **Nancy Lopez** is a nine times "rookie" winner who has both charm and charisma.

GOLFING FACTS AND FEATS

THE HIGHEST GOLF COURSE in the world is the Tuctu Golf Club in Morococha, Peru, which is 14,335 feet above sea level at its lowest point.

THE LONGEST HOLE in the world is the 7th (par 7) of the Sano Course at the Satsuki Golf Club in Japan. It measures 909 yards.

PROBABLY THE LARGEST GREEN in the world is that of the par 6 695-yard 5th hole at the International Golf Club at Bolton, Massachusetts, with an area in excess of 28,000 square feet.

THE WORLD'S LARGEST BUNKER is Hell's Half Acre on the 585-yard 7th hole of the Pine Valley Course in New Jersey.

THE WORLD'S LONGEST COURSE is the par 77 8,325-yard International at Bolton, Massachusetts, from the tiger tees.

FLOYD SATTERLEE ROOD used the United States as a course, when he played from the Pacific to the Atlantic from 14 September 1963 to 3 October 1964 in 114,737 strokes. He lost 3,511 balls on the 3,397.7-mile trail.

THE LOWEST RECORDED SCORE on an 18-hole course (more than 6,000 yards) for a woman is 62 by Mary "Mickey" Kathryn Wright on the par 71 6,286-yard Hogan Park Course at Midland, Texas, on November 1964.

THE LOWEST SCORE recorded in a first-class professional tournament on a course of more than 6,000 yards in the UK is 61 by Thomas Bruce Haliburton of Wentworth Golf Club in the Spalding Tournament at Worthing, West Sussex, in June 1952 and 61 by Peter J. Butler in the Bowmaker Tournament on the Old Course at Sunningdale, Berkshire, on 4 July 1967.

THE RECORD FOR 36 HOLES is 122 by Sam Snead in the 1959 Sam Snead Festival on 16–17 May 1959.

A DRIVE OF 2,640 YARDS across ice was achieved by an Australian meteorologist named Nils Lied at Mawson Base, Antartica, in 1962.

THE LONGEST RECORDED HOLED PUTT in a major tournament was one of 86 feet on the vast 13th green at the Augusta National in Georgia by Cary Middlecoff in the 1955 US Masters Tournament.

ROBERT TYRE "BOBBY" JONES JNR was reputed to have holed a putt in excess of 100 feet at the 5th green in the first round of the 1927 Open at St Andrews.

BOB COOK sunk a putt measured at 140 feet $2\frac{3}{4}$ inches on the 18th at St Andrews in the International Fourball Pro Am Tournament on 1 October 1976.

AT LEAST FOUR PLAYERS are recorded to have played a long course (more than 6,000 yards) in a score of 58, most recently Monte Carlo Money on the par 72 6,607-yard Las Vegas Municipal Course in Nevada on 11 March 1981.

ON THE RUNWAY at Baldonnel Military Airport in Dublin, Liam Higgins drove a Spalding Top Flite ball 634.1 yards on 25 September 1984.

THE LOWEST RECORDED SCORE on a long course in the UK is 58 by Harry Weetman, the British Ryder Cup golfer, for the 617-yard Croham Hurst Course in Croydon, Surrey, on 30 January 1956.

THE GREATEST RECORDED DRIVE on an ordinary course is one of 515 yards by Michael Hoke Austin of Los Angeles, California, in the US National Seniors Open Championship at Las Vegas, Nevada, on 25 September 1974. Austin, 6 feet 2 inches and weighing 210 pounds, drove the ball to within a yard of the green on the par 4 450-yard 5th hole of the Winterwood Course. It rolled 65 yards past the flag. He was aided by an estimated 35 mph tailwind.

THAD DABER, using a 6 iron, played the 6,037-yard Lochmore Golf Course at Cary, North Carolina, in 73 on 10 November 1985 to win the World One-Club Championship.

CHEVALIER VON CITTERN went round 18 holes in 316, averaging 17.55 per hole, at Biarritz in France in 1888.

STEVEN WARD took 222 strokes for the 6,212-yard Pecos Course in Reeves County, Texas, on 18 June 1976 – but he was aged only 3 years and 286 days!

A PLAYER in the qualifying round of the Shawnee Invitational for Ladies at Shawnee-on-Delaware, Pennsylvania, in about 1912, took 166 strokes for the short 130-yard 16th hole. Her tee shot went into the Binniekill River and the ball floated. She put out in a boat with her exemplary but statistically minded husband at the oars. She eventually beached the ball 1½ miles downstream, but was not yet out of the wood. She had to play through one on the home run.

SEVENTY-SEVEN PLAYERS completed the 18-hole 6,502-yard Kern City Course in California in 10 minutes 30 seconds on 24 August 1984 using one ball. Score – 80!

THE MOST HOLES-IN-ONE in a year is 28 by Scott Palmer from 5 June 1983 to 31 May 1984, all on par 3 and par 4 holes between 130 yards and 350 yards in length at Balboa Park in San Diego, California.

THE GREATEST NUMBER OF ROUNDS played on foot in 24 hours is 22 and five holes – a total of 401 holes – by Ian Colston, aged 35, at Bendigo Golf Club in Victoria (a par 73 6,061-yard course) on 27–28 November 1971.

A RECORD 321,779 COMPETITORS – 206,820 men and 114,959 women – played the 1984 Volkswagen Grand Prix Open Amateur Championship in the UK.

THE GREATEST MARGIN OF VICTORY in a major tournament is 21 strokes by Jerry Pate in the Columbian Open with 262 on 10–13 December 1981. Cecilia Leitch won the Canadian Ladies Open Championship in 1921 by the biggest margin for a major title – 17 up and 15 to play.

JACQUELINE ANN MERCER won her first South African title at Humewood Golf Club in Port Elizabeth in 1948 and her fourth at Port Elizabeth Golf Club on 4 May 1979, 31 years later.

THE LONGEST DELAYED RESULT in any national open championship occurred in the 1931 US Open at Toledo, Ohio. George von Elm and Billy Burke tied at 292, then tied the first replay at 149. Burke won the second replay by a single stroke after 72 extra holes.

THE LOWEST RECORDED SCORE for throwing a golf ball round 18 holes (more than 6,000 yards) is 82 by Joe Flynn, aged 21, at the 6,228-yard Port Royal Course in Bermuda on 27 March 1975.

THE LONGEST STRAIGHT HOLE ever holed in one shot is the 10th (447-yard) at Miracle Hills Golf Club at Omaha, Nebraska, by Robert Mitera on 7 October 1965. Mitera stood 5 feet 6 inches tall and weighed 165 pounds. He was a two handicap player who normally drove 245 yards. A 50 mph gust carried his shot over a 290-yard drop-off.

THE GREATEST NUMBER of holes-in-one in a career is 68 by Harry Lee Bonner from 1967 to 1985, most of them at his 9-hole home course of Las Gallinas, San Rafael, California.

THE SLOWEST STROKEPLAY TOURNAMENT round was one of 6 hours 45 minutes taken by South Africa in the first round of the 1972 World Cup at the Royal Melbourne Golf Club in Australia. This was a four-ball medal round, everything holed out.

CLUBS THROUGH THE CENTURIES

The game of golf has developed alongside the equipment. In the ancient game, clubs were much longer and flatter in design than they are today. Players gripped them in the palms of their hands and swung them flat around the body, bouncing them off their shoulders or biceps in the backswing.

The manufacture of clubs has, for many centuries, been a highly skilled affair. In 1603 we know that one William Mayne, a bowmaker by profession, was appointed clubmaker to James VI of Scotland – James I of England.

At this time clubs had shafts made of ash or hazel with a head of blackthorn, beech, apple or pear. The lie was flatter and the heads much longer than present day clubs – about 1 inch from front to back and 4 to 5 inches long in the head.

The majority of clubs were wooden, with quaint names such as playclub, brassie, grassed driver, long spoon, short spoon and bathie, which implied a personal relationship between club and player. The irons, on the other hand, were for shots from particularly difficult places – hence a bunker iron, rutt iron, track iron and so on.

Over the years the irons were used not only for recovery shots but also for general approach play. By the end of the 19th century a new range had been developed for longer shots – the mid iron, cleek, niblick and mashie, for example.

From 1948, the use of the gutty ball in place of the old-fashioned feathery ball brought a further change to the game. Players found a definite advantage when hickory was used for the shafts. They had more tautness than ash or hazel ones, allowing players to swing in a more upright stance.

The design also changed in that the shaft was now bored into a hole in the head, replacing the original method of splicing the two together.

The introduction of the rubber ball at the end of the 19th century had brought about an earlier change in the game. This ball required the use of harder wood for

durability, and persimmon was therefore used. Originally there had been no insert to the woods, but soon either bone, ivory or, later, plastic was inserted in order to impart extra strength. A shortage of good persimmon later led to experiments with laminated wood.

Persimmon still remains the most highly prized of woods for the professional and fanatical golfer. But for most players, laminates and other similar materials are now the order of the day. Hickory had been used for the shaft for some years. But with a shortage of this wood, also, after World War I, clubmakers experimented with steel shafts.

By the 1930s players were using so many clubs that caddies were suffering under the weight of carrying up to 25 clubs in huge bags. It was then that the Royal and Ancient and the United States Golf Association agreed a maximum of 14 clubs – a number still adhered to today.

27

The traditional method of making clubs is, many would argue, still the best. An old set hand-made by craftsmen is of considerable value, if in good condition. All the shaping was done by eye and the point of balance worked out on the edge of the work surface.

Early irons (right) had a flatter lie than their modern counterparts. Originally irons were used only for particularly difficult or awkward shots.

An old set of persimmon woods **(far right)**. The heads are solid, not made with inserts as they are today.

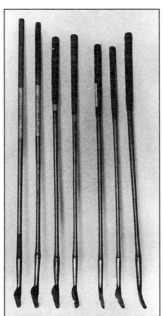

GOLF BALLS THEN AND NOW

No doubt the pioneers of golf would have regarded with disbelief the dimpled sphere that is today's golf ball. But just as the courses, clubs and rules have evolved through the years, so the golf ball has changed out of all recognition from the first ones ever used.

Three basic types of ball have figured in the development of the game – the feathery, the gutta percha and the now familiar rubber-cored ball. The latter two have been introduced within the last 150 years, but it was the feathery that was used virtually unchallenged for almost 400 years until the mid 19th century.

The feathery enjoyed such dominance not so much through any specific virtues it possessed as the fact that there was no viable alternative. This ball consisted of a spherical outer shell which was stuffed with a large quantity of feathers that had been boiled to soften them and make them more compactible. The amount used was traditionally a "top hatful", which was about 2 litres. The hole through which the feathers were rammed was sewn up and the ball was then hammered into a sphere. The process was time-consuming and very expensive, since even a skilled worker could only make three or four balls a day.

The resultant ball was beset with problems. It was rarely spherical and so would fly erratically and roll unreliably. On wet days it would soak up water, making it inconsistent in weight and so difficult to play. The water would also rot the stitching, causing the ball to split open on stoney ground.

All in all, the feathery was less than ideal for playing consistent golf. So when,

Traditionally the feathery golf ball was, as its name suggests, stuffed with feathers – the amount was enough to fill a top hat!

around 1850, the properties of a Malaysian gum called gutta percha were discovered, golfers abandoned the feathery with no reluctance.

Gutta percha could be softened in hot water, rolled into a sphere – at first by hand and later in steel moulds – and then hardened by cooling. The result was a perfect sphere that rolled true for the first time in the history of the game.

These balls were cheap and quick to make and though not as pleasant to hit as

the feathery were clearly an improvement. They occasionally shattered, but could be remoulded.

There was initially, however, a problem. The smooth balls would not fly any distance. This at first irritated the users of the so-called gutties and raised a glimmer of hope for the makers of the feathery balls who were understandably concerned at this innovation.

Eventually it was noticed that if a ball was dented during play it then flew better. Thus the gutty users began hammering dents into their balls – inadvertently establishing the principle of

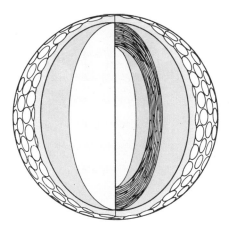

The typical composition of a modern golf ball **(above)** – a two-piece **(left)** and a three-piece **(right)** with Surlyn cover.

The development of the golf ball **(below)** from left to right: feathery, smooth gutty, chiselled gutty, machined gutty, bramble, lattice, early dimpled and the new DDH (dodecahedron) with 12 identical pentagonal sides. This ball has 10 equators without touching a dimple.

the modern dimpled ball. The gutty now flew perfectly and became the standard ball for the next 50 years.

At the turn of the century a man named Coburn Haskell introduced the soft-cored elastic wound ball from which the modern version evolved. Initially wrapped in gutta percha, this ball was livelier and more resilient. But, despite these qualities, it was regarded with suspicion and the authorities seriously discussed banning it.

This all changed, however, during a practice round at the 1902 British Open between the professional Alexander Herd and the gifted amateur John Ball. Herd should have won easily but found himself consistently outplayed, both on the fairway and the green. Ball was using one of the new balls. Herd was invited to try one and remarkably went on to win the championship. Naturally the ball became an overnight success.

Since then the rubber-cored ball has become the standard for all golfers. Despite wrangles over the weight and size that began after World War I, a decision was finally reached in 1968 that in any PGA competition worldwide, the American standard of 1.68 inches diameter only would be admissable.

Modern technology continues to play its part in the development of the golf ball, making it increasingly more consistent both in flight and roll. Other refinements have included polymer coatings and the introduction of solid and semi-solid balls. Also the pattern and number of dimples has been changed, together with variations in the compression to suit individual players and conditions.

GOLF CLUBS

Although in the past there was no restriction on the number of clubs you could carry around a golf course, this is now limited to 14, including a putter. There is still an element of choice, however, since manufacturers produce five woods and 11 irons, as well as a selection of putters in different styles.

For the average club golfer, the ideal full set would be as follows: a driver (1 wood) and 3 and 4 woods; 2, 3, 4, 5, 6, 7, 8 and 9 irons; a pitching wedge and a sand wedge; and finally a putter.

When starting to play, beginners were once often advised to get a half-set. This normally comprised a driver and 3 wood, then either the odd or even numbered irons. The idea was to complete the set by buying the other clubs at a later date. Unfortunately this is no longer really practical since clubmakers are forever changing models and designs and the one thing you must ensure is that your clubs match each other, both in balance and weight.

When buying a set of clubs, always discuss it with your local professional first. Not only will he advise you on the clubs best suited for you, but can also regrip and repair the ones you choose.

Drivers are made with a loft of anything between 7 and 12 degrees. While good players may be happy with a 7-degree loft, the club player should find the driver easier to use with a little more loft.

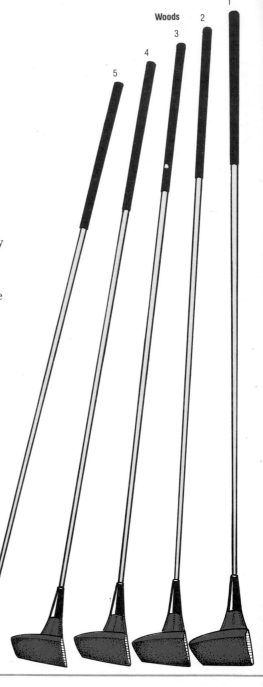

Woods
1
2
3
4
5

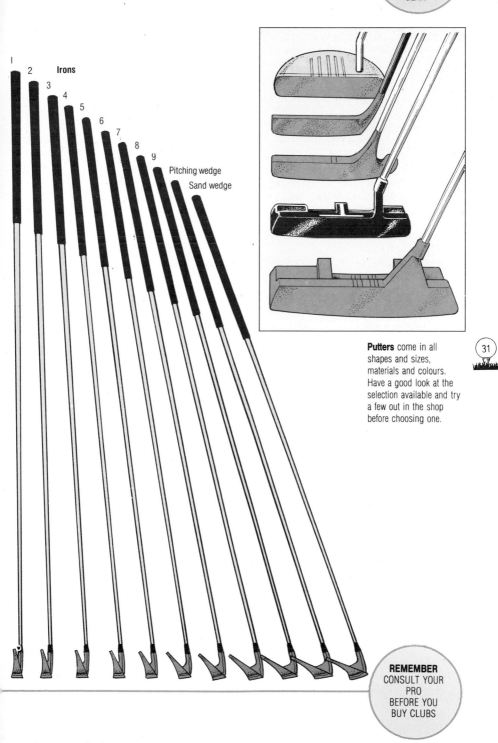

Irons

1
2
3
4
5
6
7
8
9

Pitching wedge

Sand wedge

Putters come in all shapes and sizes, materials and colours. Have a good look at the selection available and try a few out in the shop before choosing one.

31

DESIGN OF CLUBS

Knowing how golf clubs are designed will help you select the ones that are best for you. Choose a club with a suitable shaft. With irons, this can be less important than with woods. With the driver, the correct shaft is essential. If using a shaft that is too stiff, the tendency is for poor height and shots finishing to the right. If the shaft is too weak and flexible, it may lead to erratic direction.

Shafts are generally graded as follows: S = stiff, R = regular men's, A = amateur (older men and top-class women) and L = ladies'. Some shafts are graduated more in numbers, but your professional can tell you how this numbering relates to the regular men's and ladies' shafts. Don't use a stiff shaft unless you are sure you can really cope with it.

The regular men's shaft is suitable for almost all male club players. The ladies' shaft is right for most women. Taller women golfers using a longer shaft are advised to choose the A shaft and not the regular men's one. Similarly, a tall man may need a stiff shaft with extra length.

32

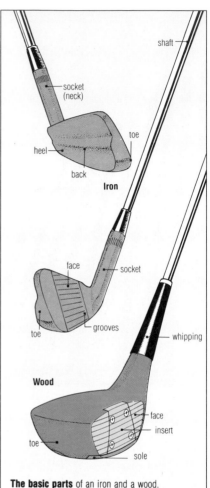

The basic parts of an iron and a wood.

LOOK AFTER YOUR CLUBS
Whether metal or wood, protect your clubs with headcovers. If they get wet, remove the covers when you have finished playing and dry them. Keep woods in good condition by touching up with polythene varnish any area where the seal has been damaged. If the face is badly marked, apply a small drop of linseed oil and allow it to dry before adding the varnish.

The grip on a club is generally rubber or leather. As a rule it is slightly egg-shaped and not perfectly round, with a slight ridge at the back of the shaft.

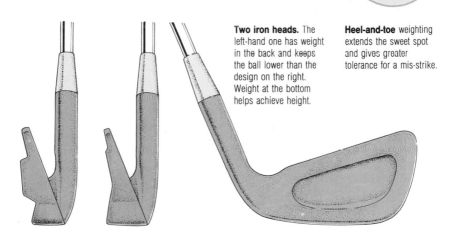

Two iron heads. The left-hand one has weight in the back and keeps the ball lower than the design on the right. Weight at the bottom helps achieve height.

Heel-and-toe weighting extends the sweet spot and gives greater tolerance for a mis-strike.

The type of irons you use can dictate the height you get with shots. With weight at the bottom of the clubhead, the ball will tend to fly high; with weight at the back, the ball tends to go lower.

Tournament professionals will usually use the latter type, although these are not necessarily right for the club player. They require a very good strike, particularly with the long irons.

Irons come either with a standard blade, in which the weight is evenly distributed along the clubhead, or with heel-to-toe weighting, such as the design of Pings. This extends the sweet spot and gives a larger hitting area, being more forgiving if the ball is struck off-centre on the clubface.

Iron heads can either be made of stainless steel, which will wear indefinitely, or mild steel and chrome plating, which can produce better feel and are therefore preferred by tournament players. But they do not have the durability of stainless steel. Again, ask your professional for advice.

33

The angle of loft increases through the set of woods and irons to allow progressively higher shots. There is a $\frac{1}{2}$ inch difference in length for adjacent clubs – sometimes $\frac{1}{4}$ inch with short irons. This change in length is combined with a grading to the lie. The pitching wedge sits the most upright of the irons, with the long irons and the woods the flattest. The lie does have to be varied for taller and shorter players.

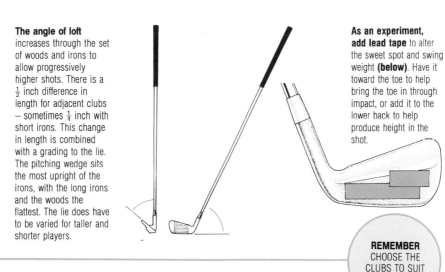

As an experiment, add lead tape to alter the sweet spot and swing weight **(below)**. Have it toward the toe to help bring the toe in through impact, or add it to the lower back to help produce height in the shot.

REMEMBER
CHOOSE THE
CLUBS TO SUIT
YOUR GAME

CLUBS TO SUIT YOU

Your choice of golf clubs is vital. It does not mean buying very expensive equipment, but it does mean having clubs set up to suit your height, strength and general game.

In theory, most players can use clubs of a fairly standard length. Although our height varies enormously, most people's hands hang at about the same distance off the ground. Men from 5 feet 2 inches to 5 feet 10 inches can normally use standard length clubs – and so too can women from 5 feet to 5 feet 5 inches.

The point to remember is that if you add length to the club, the shaft becomes whippier and the head feels heavier. If you shorten a club, it becomes stiffer and there is usually less feel to the head. Tall players, in particular, will often have difficulty with clubs that are too short, especially through the shorter irons.

The set of irons should normally be graduated by $\frac{1}{2}$ inch between each one. But for the tall player, graduating the clubs by $\frac{1}{4}$ inch from the 6 iron through the wedges often overcomes any difficulties.

Also vital is having the correct lie to clubs – in other words, the angle at which the club sits to the ground when the player takes up his stance. As you hit the ball, the shaft flexes, the hands may rise and the sole of the club comes through flat on the ground.

If the player is short, holds his hands low at address or has clubs set up incorrectly, where the toe of the club is off the ground at address, the tendency is for the heel to drag into the ground and the clubface to close. As a result the shot is pulled or drawn. In other words, the club is too upright. This is often not a problem for the club player, however, and may indeed help him eliminate any tendency he has to slice.

If the player is tall, or holds his hands high at address, the heel of the club may be up and the toe may tend to dig into the ground. This is disastrous and will cause

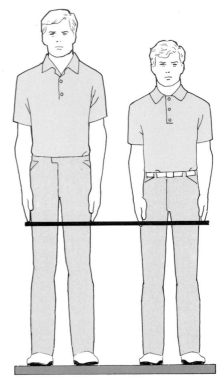

The length of clubs does not need to vary as much as you might imagine. Whether you are tall or short, fingertips come to roughly the same level. Men over 5 feet 10 inches may need longer clubs and women under 5 feet shorter ones. The standard men's length of club is 1 inch longer than that of the women's throughout the whole set.

a slice. So any tall player must check the lie of his clubs very carefully.

Always buy a set of irons that can be changed, that is one in which the iron neck can be bent. Woods cannot generally be altered. And always seek the advice of a professional golfer, particularly if you are tall, and don't just buy off-the-peg from a local store.

Buy clubs with the correct thickness of grip, and use a grip in which the fingers of the left hand just barely touch the pad of the left thumb without digging in. Keep

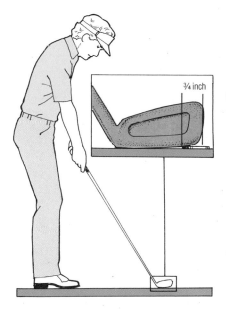

Tall players may find standard clubs sit toward the toe, with the heel up **(above)**. This is disastrous and produces a slice. Equally, if the club sits excessively on its heel it may produce a pull/hook. If a club sits correctly, you can expect to slide a small coin about ¾ inch under the toe **(left)**.

grips in good condition by washing them regularly with warm water. And ensure they are put back on straight, with any line down the front of the grip perfectly square to the clubface.

If you buy a new set of clubs with poorly fitted grips, ask your professional to change them. The grip on a club is not round, but egg-shaped. So if they are not set on correctly, you will find difficulty in holding the clubface square and returning it squarely to the ball.

The experienced golfer should be able to pick up a club, close his eyes, twiddle it round and set his hands squarely on – just from the feel of the grip.

A round-soled club (below) is more adaptable to different slopes and easier to play with than one with a flat sole **(bottom)**.

35

The thickness of grip is crucial to good stroke-making. Minor adjustments can be made by wrapping tape around the shaft.

tape

REMEMBER
CORRECT LIE
TO CLUBS
IS VITAL

PUTTERS

Almost all professionals use a putter with a flat-fronted grip. It encourages the correct hold – thumbs to the front and hands to the side. The rules say that there must be at least 10 degrees between the putter shaft and the vertical. This is to stop players using a croquet-type action, facing the hole.

Theoretically, the more upright your putter sits, the easier it is to swing back and through on a straight line with a hingeing action. If you have a putter that sits flat, you will tend to swing it around in a curve. So upright is generally easiest.

Always check the sweet spot on the putter. That is the hitting area on the clubface that will give you a reliable strike. To see just how good it is, hold the putter up loosely from the top of the shaft with your left hand and start tapping along the face from the toe with a coin or fingernail.

Tap at the toe and you will feel it twist. Gradually work toward the middle of the face and you will feel it wanting to swing back and through with no twist. Tap again toward the heel and you will feel it twist once more. The bigger the area with no twist, the easier the putter is to use.

Mark the centre of the sweet spot and aim to hit the ball from this. Marks put on by the manufacturers do not always correspond with the sweet spot. Check this before buying one.

Putters basically fall into four designs – the blade, the mallet, the centre shaft and the Ping type with a heel and toe design. The last two are likely to have the largest

A fairly upright putter (left) of the correct length encourages a good stroke. A flat lie, or one that is too long, can produce a poor, wristy action.

Choose a putter with a flat-fronted grip **(right)** to encourage yourself to hold it correctly. And remember – a putter has to sit at least 10 degrees from the vertical. Upright ones tend to be easier to use **(far right)**.

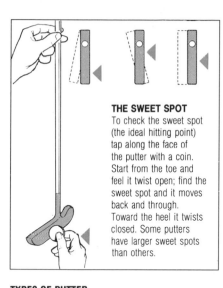

THE SWEET SPOT
To check the sweet spot (the ideal hitting point) tap along the face of the putter with a coin. Start from the toe and feel it twist open; find the sweet spot and it moves back and through. Toward the heel it twists closed. Some putters have larger sweet spots than others.

sweet spots. By comparison with these, the old-fashioned blade putter can be difficult to use.

The length of putters varies from about 32 inches to 36 inches. If your putter is too long, the temptation is to hold it at the top of the shaft and over-bend the wrists. Good putting requires the left wrist to ride high. The correct length of shaft will encourage this.

Putters vary slightly in loft – from 3 degrees to about 7 degrees. Those with very little loft are ideal for tournament greens. Those with more loft can be useful on bad greens and for players who press their hands forward at address. A light putter can be very difficult to control, while a heavy putter tends to encourage a smooth swing.

TYPES OF PUTTER

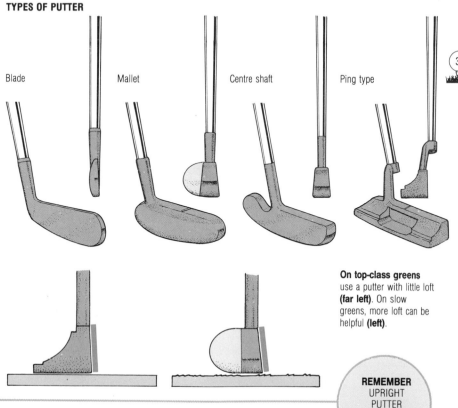

Blade   Mallet   Centre shaft   Ping type

On top-class greens
use a putter with little loft **(far left)**. On slow greens, more loft can be helpful **(left)**.

REMEMBER
UPRIGHT PUTTER WITH LARGE SWEET SPOT

THE GOLFER'S CLOTHING: 1

Golf clothing should not just be smart; most importantly it needs to be comfortable and functional. There are no specific rules relating to general dress on the course, although most established clubs do set basic standards and you should always respect these.

You need to wear clothes that allow you totally free movement of the various parts of the body essential to the basic shots. There is no shortage of choice when it comes to shirts, pullovers, trousers, shorts, slacks and skirts.

Bear in mind that you will be out on the course for several hours at a time, during which there may well be a dramatic change in conditions. If the weather looks changeable, make sure you have sufficient extra clothing to keep warm, since cold limbs and joints are your worst enemy when playing golf, and pack waterproofs in your golf bag in case it rains.

When choosing waterproofs, remember that you are unlikely to find any garment that is totally impervious to water. The

cheapest rainwear is usually lightweight nylon, which although not particularly smart does have the advantage of being compact enough to fit into any bag.

At the other end of the market is the expensive breatheable fabric suit, such as that made from Gortex. This takes up far more space in your bag and tends to be more suitable if you are likely to play a complete round in the rain.

Whichever waterproofs you choose, look for trousers with legs wide enough to go easily over golf shoes, preferably with

zips at the bottom of the legs which you can tighten to prevent the bottoms flapping around in the wind. Ensure that the jacket is loose enough to allow you to swing freely and try to get one with as few seams as possible. Another point to remember is that you want a suit that does not make a lot of noise as you move in the shot.

Headwear is also important, particularly when it is windy, since you do not want to be distracted by your hair blowing in your face and eyes. Here

THE GOLFER'S CLOTHING: 2

again, there is a wide range, from caps to cloth hats. Equally, on a fine day you need to keep the sun out of your eyes, and a peaked cap or visor is very useful.

Whatever you wear on your head, make sure it fits comfortably and does not keep slipping or flopping about as you move through the shot.

A sound pair of shoes is essential for firm gripping and good footwork. The most expensive tend to have leather uppers and leather soles with spikes. But these can be very stiff and, if the soles do not bend freely, you can end up with blisters at the back of your feet.

The ideal combination for most players is a leather upper, which will breathe, combined with a rubber sole with either spikes or "pimples". Again, the soles need

to be suitably flexible to encourage good footwork. Stiff soles can not only be uncomfortable but can also cause problems in the swing.

Look for shoes with solid toe caps. This again encourages good footwork for the right foot to come through on to the end of the toes. Shoes that are too flexible will not give proper support.

Also bear in mind that the heel height can vary slightly and this can affect balance and legwork. Highish heels can push the weight forward on to the ball of the left foot through impact, instead of allowing you to get back on to the heel.

When you buy a pair of spiked shoes, loosen all the spikes and drop in a little easing oil to prevent them rusting in.

Most players wear a left-hand glove to

Rubber-soled shoes with pimples **(right)** are more flexible than those made entirely of leather.

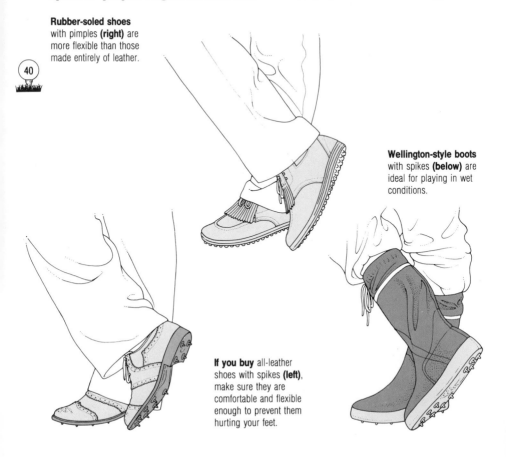

Wellington-style boots with spikes **(below)** are ideal for playing in wet conditions.

If you buy all-leather shoes with spikes **(left)**, make sure they are comfortable and flexible enough to prevent them hurting your feet.

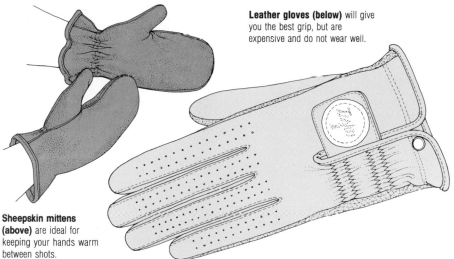

Leather gloves (below) will give you the best grip, but are expensive and do not wear well.

Sheepskin mittens (above) are ideal for keeping your hands warm between shots.

encourage a constant grip. Leather tends to be expensive and, although giving arguably the best feel, may not be as durable as some of the best synthetics. A glove with an extra pad at the base of the hand can reduce wear and tear. It should fit more tightly than a normal glove.

Take care when putting your glove on; slide it on the fingers and thumb, rather than pulling it on from the wrist.

In winter, wearing a pair of thick mittens over your golf glove is usually easier than playing in a pair of gloves. Special trolley mitts are available to cover both the trolley handle and your hands.

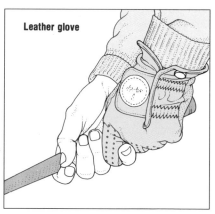

Leather glove

41

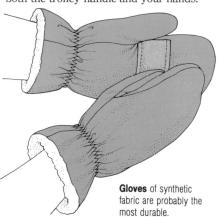

Gloves of synthetic fabric are probably the most durable.

You can buy special mitts that fit on to your golf trolley.

THE GOLFER'S KIT: 1

The list of items that form the golfer's kit grows longer and longer as new products – some quite useful and others purely gimmicks – come on the market. When you are starting or want to build up the essential kit, only buy what you really need or will find helpful.

The items included here represent a guide to help you choose the most practical as well as essential.

Golf bags

These were first introduced and used around 1870. Before then, the players' caddies simply carried the clubs in a bundle under their arms. Now a golf bag is an essential and you are unlikely to be allowed on a course without one. Needless to say, the bags come in a whole range of shapes and sizes.

● Drainpipe carry bag – ideal for six or seven clubs and when practising. There is no room for extra clothing.

● Light carry bags – make sure the strap is strong enough for the number of clubs you intend to carry. If fully collapsible, it may be unsuitable for a full set and cannot be used with a trolley.

● Carry/trolley bag – get one small enough to carry, but large enough for a full set – and rigid so you can use it on a trolley. Again, a strong strap is essential. Look for one with a hood for protection in the rain.

● Supadivida bag – with compartments for each club. Good for keeping clubs apart, particularly for graphite shafted ones that can be heavy.

● Tournament bag – needs a very strong strap and a strong base, since caddies tend to sit on it!

● All-in-one bag/trolley – ideal when travelling and for packing in the car.

Look for a bag with a good, strong strap suitable for the number of clubs you want to carry around, a stiff bag if you want it for trolley use, a hood for the rain, a stout base and enough pocket space for anything you are likely to want to take on the course with you.

42

1

2

3

4

5

6

7

Holdalls

These are available with zip-off ends for storing valuables. It is also a good idea to get one that has a section for shoes, to keep them separate from your clothing.

Headcovers

These can be made of vinyl, fabric, leather or sheepskin. Although expensive, sheepskin is in many ways the best since it is waterproof and will also breathe, preventing moisture building up inside. Vinyl tends to retain moisture.

Iron covers are very useful for keeping your set in pristine condition. But unless your irons are of stainless steel, make sure the covers are not holding moisture.

A selection of useful golfer's kit
1 Umbrella
2 Large holdall
3 Holdall with zip-off ends
4 Light carry bag
5 Practice ball bag
6 Practice ball tube
7 Headcovers
8 Tournament bag with waterproof cover
9 All-in-one bag
10 Flight case
11 Drainpipe carry bag
12 Carry/trolley bag
13 General purpose towel for cleaning
14 Individual plastic club separator tubes

THE GOLFER'S KIT: 2

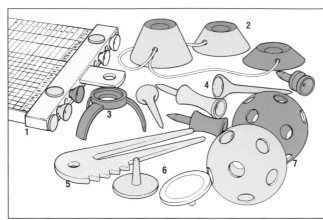

The following are essential parts of the golfer's equipment:
1 Tee holder with score card and ball markers
2 Rubber castle tees at set heights for different clubs
3 Plastic castle tee
4 Selection of wooden and plastic tees
5 Pitchfork to repair pitchmarks made on the surface of the green
6 Ball markers
7 Practice balls

Essential accessories

You will need a lot of other items for use around the course. These include a bag towel for cleaning the ball, drying your hands and so on when it is wet. Get a good umbrella that is both lightning and windproof. With this type, the frame can be pulled about quite roughly and will stand up to a near gale.

Tees can be wooden or plastic. Wooden ones will break on almost every drive, but some professionals suggest they do less damage to the clubs, particularly good persimmon drivers, than plastic ones. For the club player, castle tees of set height are an excellent idea. Use one height for drivers, another for a 3 or 4 wood and the shortest for an iron tee shot.

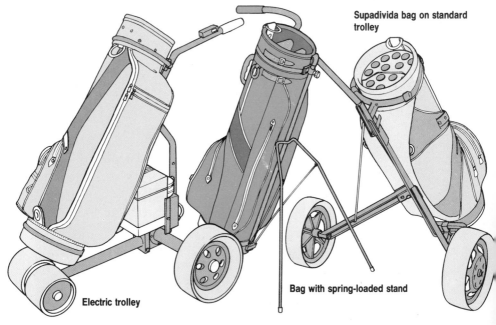

Supadivida bag on standard trolley

Bag with spring-loaded stand

Electric trolley

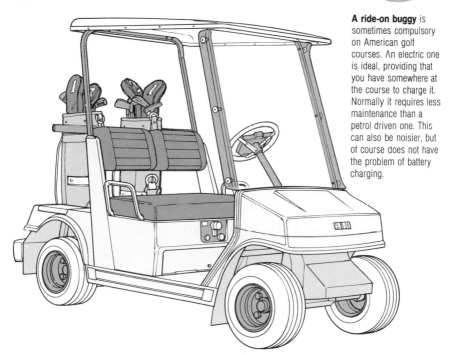

A ride-on buggy is
sometimes compulsory
on American golf
courses. An electric one
is ideal, providing that
you have somewhere at
the course to charge it.
Normally it requires less
maintenance than a
petrol driven one. This
can also be noisier, but
of course does not have
the problem of battery
charging.

45

Most professionals simply play with a pocket full of tees. More practical is a tee holder which will also take a pencil, your scorecard and some ball markers. You can get ones that fasten on to your golf bag.

A ball washer that stays moist is a real boon and particularly useful on courses where there are few ball washers beside the tees. Although this item is not used by professionals, who usually rely on spit and polish from the caddies, it is useful for the amateur and saves the potential hazard of licking the ball.

Add to your kit a ball retriever for fishing stray balls out of water and a practice ball bag or tube for use on the practice ground.

Trolleys
Most players use a trolley, whether a handcart or an electric model. With a hand trolley, check how small it is when folded up, and consider whether or not you want to remove the bag from the trolley before folding it to pack in the car.

Some players prefer to leave the two attached, while others find this too heavy and bulky and prefer to separate them.

Check not only the weight of the trolley but also the way it pulls. A trolley needs to be well balanced so that it is comfortable – whether you are pulling or pushing it. Ideally you want to be able to pull it with your arm hanging relaxed at your side. If the balance is wrong or the handle too long, your arm can be forced to hold it at an awkward angle.

Look for one with an adjustable handle and try out the trolley in the shop with your own bag of clubs on it.

With an electric trolley, consider its weight and that of the battery. Many older players have electric trolleys for ease of use on the course and then find the battery is too heavy to lift into the car. Always buy an electric trolley from your own professional. You may need to call on him to recharge the battery, a job he may not be too sympathetic about if you bought the equipment elsewhere.

DYNAMICS OF BALL AND CLUB

A sound understanding of the dynamics of ball and club is essential if you want to improve your game. Without this, learning is just trial and error. Most club golfers watch their shots fly off to the right or left without really knowing why this has happened.

The first thing to appreciate is that a golf ball is designed to take up spin. The dimples on the surface encourage spin to help get the ball airborne. In taking up backspin, the ball also takes up sidespin with great ease.

In most ball games, the ball flies straight and you learn to put spin on to make it curve. In golf you first have to learn to take sidespin off the ball to get it flying straight. Then the good player learns to put spin on to bend the ball as required. This is done either to curve

shots or to hold them into the wind.

The more lofted the club, the greater the backspin and the less sidespin you get. It is difficult, for example, to bend a ball with a 9 iron. In contrast, the driver produces little backspin but easily effects sidespin, so any hook or slice is exaggerated.

The other principle to understand is that, provided the ball is struck from the middle or near middle of the clubface, it starts in the direction of the swing.

A correctly struck ball starting left is produced by a left-aimed swing – out-to-in. It may then bend left or right, depending on the clubface angle.

Analyse any shot in terms of "Where did it start? How did it curve?" and you will quickly begin to get a clue to any fault in the swing.

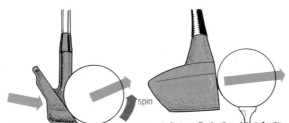

46

THE STRAIGHT SHOT
Attack and clubface both on target at the moment of impact. The swing path starts it straight. A square clubface keeps the ball flying with no sidespin.

The loft of the iron naturally gets the clubface beneath the back of the ball **(left)** and produces backspin. The drive is the one shot struck on the upswing **(right)**. This starts it off at the correct trajectory, with just the right degree of backspin.

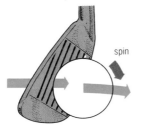

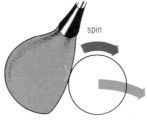

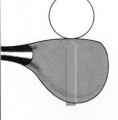

Lofted clubs hit the ball at the bottom **(left)**, producing backspin and little sidespin. Straightfaced clubs hit the ball near its equator **(right)**, producing lots of sidespin, if the clubface is open or closed.

The fade
The ball starts on target, drifting away slightly to the right from an open clubface. Professionals often fade a ball into the green, aiming fractionally left to allow for this. The ball stops well.

The push fade
An in-to-out attack starts the ball right of the target. An open clubface sees it bend farther right. The fault may be the left leg blocking movement, a weak grip or stiff wrists.

The slice
An out-to-in swing starts the ball left and also imparts cutspin to the shot. The clubface is open in relation to the path of the swing. Lack of turn back and stiffness through.

The push
An in-to-out attack, with the clubface square. The ball flies straight right. Often the good player's bad shot. Look at alignment and leg block through impact.

47

The draw
The clubface is fractionally closed in relation to the direction of the swing. This may be on target, with the clubface slightly left – or the clubface on target with the swing slightly right. Many think this the perfect shot.

The pull hook
A ball starting left from an out-to-in swing with a closed clubface bending it even farther. Often a poor grip and very right-handed action. Players often aim right to counteract this and imagine they hook.

The hook
A shot starting right (from a square stance) from an in-to-out swing, with the clubface closed in relation to this. Closely linked to the push. Look for the ball too far back, legs blocking movement and fast hands and wrists.

The pull
An out-to-in attack starting the ball left, with the clubface square to this path, so producing a straight left shot. Often the ball is too far forward and there is insufficient turn.

REMEMBER
TAKE SPIN OFF, THEN PUT IT BACK ON

THE SIMPLE SWING

The basic golf swing is so simple that a child of eight can do it. Unfortunately most adults can't! As with other sports, the technique for the beginner should be simple and straightforward and become complicated only for players aiming for higher standards.

The difficulty with golf is not in the swing itself, but in the strike and in the precision required to make accurate contact with the ball. Direction, too, has to be controlled because of the vast distances you have to cover. The swing is simple; keep it that way.

The problem for the beginner is that the ball is ridiculously small; the clubhead is not very big, either; the ball sits on the ground and the ground gets in the way.

With other sports, ball contact is a lot easier. In tennis, hockey or squash, for example, you have a larger weapon which makes the task of striking the ball quite straightforward. You also have just one weapon in your hand the whole time and grow to feel confident with it.

But in golf you have to choose different clubs and feel comfortable with each one straight away. A further problem is that the stationary golf ball allows you too much time for thinking. It enables you to analyse the swing and think too much of the body movements. Compare the swing to hitting a tennis ball and see how easy that can be. Let the golf swing be simple.

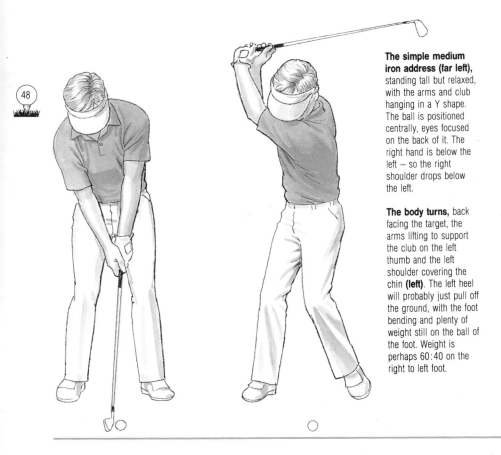

The simple medium iron address (far left), standing tall but relaxed, with the arms and club hanging in a Y shape. The ball is positioned centrally, eyes focused on the back of it. The right hand is below the left — so the right shoulder drops below the left.

The body turns, back facing the target, the arms lifting to support the club on the left thumb and the left shoulder covering the chin **(left).** The left heel will probably just pull off the ground, with the foot bending and plenty of weight still on the ball of the foot. Weight is perhaps 60:40 on the right to left foot.

SIMPLE SWING EXERCISES
The simple swing involves turning your body to the right and then the left, and combining this with lifting the arms — up, down, up. Try this without the club. As your body turns, the weight transfers.

Add the arm lift, first with your hands apart and then palms together, forcing the right arm to fold going back and the left arm to fold going through. Add the club and you can feel the simple swing taking shape.

The body is turning through to face the target, the arms swishing the club down and up, collecting the ball on the way **(far left)**. The left heel has pushed firmly back on to the ground, eyes still focused on the ball at impact — and for a split second seeing the ground that it sat on.

Finishing the simple swing, facing the target, with the club resting neatly on the left shoulder **(left)**. The whole body from knees, hips, elbows to eyes is on target. The knees more or less touch, the right foot spinning on to the tips of the toes.

49

REMEMBER
THE CONTACT
IS HARD
BUT THE SWING
IS SIMPLE

THE GRIP

The grip is all-important. It controls the height, length and direction of your shots and can make or break your game.

Rest the clubhead on the ground, with the bottom groove facing your target. Hang the left hand loosely beside the club before folding it over to take hold of the club (**1** and **2**). The tip of the thumb and joint of the index finger should be roughly level, with the line between the thumb and index finger pointing up to your right ear or shoulder (**3**).

Add the right hand, with the palm behind the club, which should be resting in the finger tips. Fold the hand over, with the left thumb in the pocket of the right hand. The index finger is separated slightly from the next in a trigger

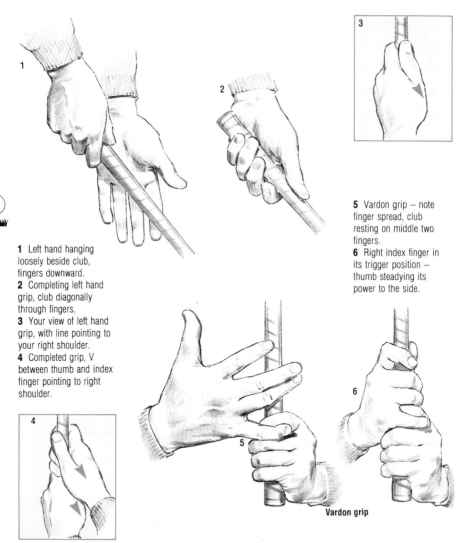

1 Left hand hanging loosely beside club, fingers downward.
2 Completing left hand grip, club diagonally through fingers.
3 Your view of left hand grip, with line pointing to your right shoulder.
4 Completed grip, V between thumb and index finger pointing to right shoulder.

5 Vardon grip — note finger spread, club resting on middle two fingers.
6 Right index finger in its trigger position — thumb steadying its power to the side.

Vardon grip

position, with the right thumb to the left – *never* to the front. The V between them points to the right shoulder (**4**).

Ideally use the Vardon grip, with the right little finger overlapping the left index finger (**5** and **6**). If you find this impossible because your hands are too small, use the interlocking grip (**7**) or the baseball grip with no overlap (**8**).

Faulty grips

If the left hand is too much on top of the club or the right hand too much beneath it, you will tend to return the clubface in a closed, left-aimed position. The shot will be low and hooked to the left. If both hands are too far round to the left, the grip is weakened, the club face open and the shot weak and sliced to the right.

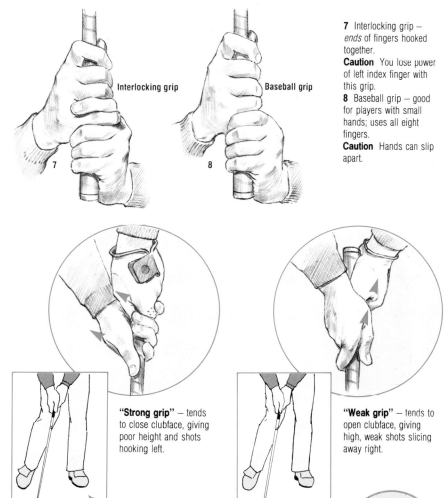

Interlocking grip

Baseball grip

7

8

7 Interlocking grip – *ends* of fingers hooked together.
Caution You lose power of left index finger with this grip.
8 Baseball grip – good for players with small hands; uses all eight fingers.
Caution Hands can slip apart.

51

"Strong grip" – tends to close clubface, giving poor height and shots hooking left.

"Weak grip" – tends to open clubface, giving high, weak shots slicing away right.

REMEMBER
GRIP LIGHTLY,
BUT DON'T
LET GO!

THE STANCE

With the stance (or address position) you are preparing your body to move, setting the plane of swing for a good contact and aiming the shot. Even good players have more trouble producing a consistent stance than any other part of their game.

The front view shows the key points: feet, shoulder width (women think "hip width"), left foot out a little, right almost straight, knees knocked in, weight on the insides of the feet. The arms hang in a Y shape, with the right hand below the left, pulling the right shoulder down – but not forward. The arms are relaxed, the wrists dropped and the head high, with the eyes looking down the face.

From behind the shot you can see the posture and distance from the ball. You must stand up straight, bottom out, and feel springy on the balls of your feet. Don't sit and sag. You must bend from the top of the legs and not from the waist.

The general rule is to stand as close as possible, with the arms hanging loose and the bottom out; but feel enough space to swing the arms back past the right hip and through beneath the chin.

Ball position

Professionals say they play all shots opposite the left heel. In fact, most don't. And this does not suit club golfers. Your swing with irons will fall opposite your nose – the centre of the stance – so play the ball there. If you are young and good, you can play it farther left!

Perfect stance – weight on inside of feet, knees in, arms relaxed, head high enough to see forward, feet shoulder width (hips for ladies).

52

Perfect posture – up tall, bottom out, springy on balls of feet, bending from top of legs, angle in between club and arms.

DON'T
sit and sag

Stand as close as you can, giving yourself enough room to swing comfortably past your right hip and beneath your chin. The taller you are, the closer you can stand, with the club more upright. Shorter people need to stand farther away.

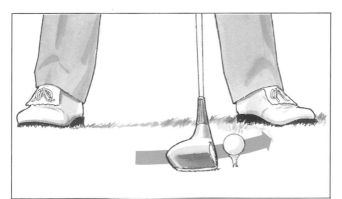

With the driver, or when you have a very good lie with a long iron or wood, play the ball forward in the stance and sweep it upward. Take care to keep the right shoulder correctly below the left at address. Don't let it be pulled forward.

53

For recovery shots and very bad or downhill lies, play the ball farther back in the stance for a steep, downward attack. The beginner should start by playing all short irons just behind centre to encourage a downward, ball then divot contact.

REMEMBER
HOWEVER TALL,
STAND UP.
DON'T SIT
AND SAG

LINING UP FOR LONG SHOTS

With most long shots you need a square stance, with the line across the feet, knees, hips, shoulders and eyes parallel to your proposed shot. It sounds easy, but it isn't. Lining up can be an optical illusion. Many golfers repeatedly aim right and hit right or compensate and pull left.

The easiest way of aiming is to choose a spot 18 inches ahead of the ball on line to the target and set the clubface to aim over this, with your feet parallel to the line from the ball to this spot.

The other common error is to open your shoulders, that is to aim them left.

This is caused by your right hand pulling the shoulder forward, or by turning as you look at the target or by having the ball too far left in the stance. This encourages you to cut across the ball with a slicing action. As a result, the shot curves away to the right.

The shoulders are often more crucial than the feet, so keep them square or fractionally closed.

The ball position is linked to direction. With the ball too far back, you may push it right. If it is too far forward, you are likely to start it to the left.

The open stance is one in which the direction of the clubface and stance diverge or open up to the target. If used unintentionally, this leads to slicing. However, it does have its uses for playing cut shots and some short finesse shots.

With the closed stance, the clubface is on target (or to the left), with the feet to the right. The swing and clubface converge, encouraging hookspin, with the ball flying to the left. This is used for bending the ball from right to left.

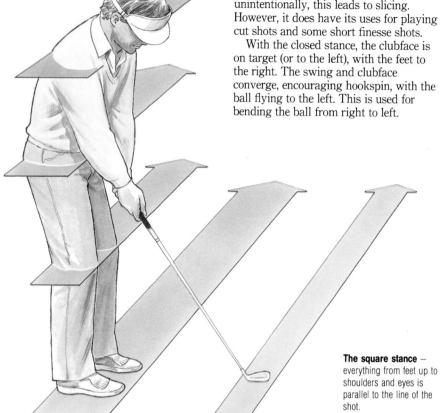

The square stance – everything from feet up to shoulders and eyes is parallel to the line of the shot.

54

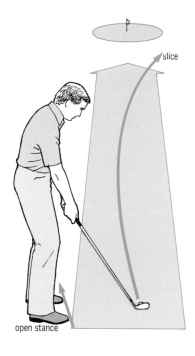

open stance

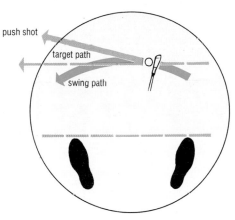

push shot

target path

swing path

The open stance (left) — clubface on target, feet and shoulders lining up to the left, encouraging a slice. The ball curves out to the right.

Playing the ball too far back in the stance **(above)**, encouraging a push shot. The ball flies off target out to the right.

55

hook

pull shot

closed stance

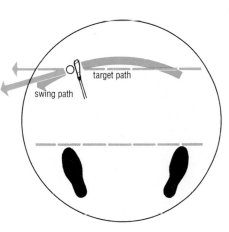

target path

swing path

The closed stance (left) — clubface on target, feet and shoulders lining up to the right, encouraging a hook.

Playing the ball too far forward in the stance **(above)**, encouraging a pull shot.

REMEMBER
PRACTISE
AIMING —
EYES CAN
FOOL YOU

THE BACKSWING

Ideally, your left arm and left side of your body should control the backswing. Start the backswing with a turn of your left shoulder, the weight transferring on to the right heel and ball of the left foot. This brings the club back on a curve.

At around hip height the beginner needs to feel the left thumb and toe of the club moving upward, with the wrists hingeing upward and the left arm lifting and drawing across the body toward the right shoulder.

By the top of the backswing, the back has turned to the target, the clubshaft is horizontal and pointing parallel to the proposed shot, and the left thumb is

supporting the club. Ideally, the clubface and left arm should be parallel on the same plane.

The good golfer will gradually add a little backward (as well as upward) hingeing of the wrists in the takeaway until, as an expert, a flat back to the left wrist is achieved at the top of the swing.

A common fault is to dip the left shoulder rather than turn it. Ideally the left arm should swing across the body, the left shoulder covering the chin, with the right arm folding into a right angle and the wrist hingeing backward. The right arm should adopt a similar position to that of a waiter carrying a tray.

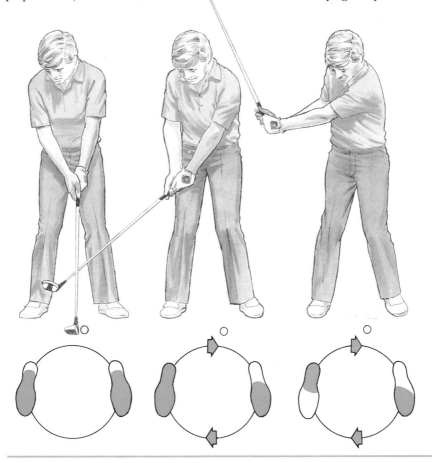

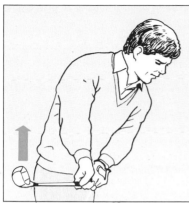

HINGE WRISTS
The beginner needs to turn into a "toe-up" position at hip height. From here the wrists can hinge up. For the good golfer the wrists do not just hinge upward. The right wrist also hinges back on itself. Combined with a flat left wrist, this gives real power.

57

For the better golfer, the right wrist hinges back in the swing into this type of position.

Dominant left side
The backswing needs to feel left side dominant. The left shoulder turns. The left arm is drawn across the chest as it lifts. The left hand (for right-handers) needs to feel in control. The weight turns round toward the right heel and the ball of the left foot.

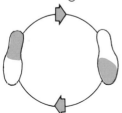

REMEMBER
LOOK FOR
LEFT SIDE
CONTROL

THE THROUGHSWING

If you drive a fast car, you need to know how to put the brakes on. If you fly a plane, you need to know how to land it. If you swing a golf club well, it will travel at over 100 miles an hour and you therefore need to learn a follow-through to stop it safely every time.

Professionals all finish with the club safely on the left shoulder or the back of the neck. Club golfers often allow their heads to get in the way of the swing and either slow down prematurely or lose their balance.

In the start of the downswing, take things slowly to give yourself time to bring the club into reverse. And

remember – the longer the club, the more crucial the timing.

Push your weight back on to the left heel and turn the body through to achieve balance on the left heel and right toes. At the same time, swish the arms and club down and up the other side, bringing the club smoothly to rest on the left shoulder. Hold this finish. Then let your arms and the club down, but keep the legs balanced.

Footwork and balance are vital. With poor balance you cannot safely achieve optimum clubhead speed. The feet should not roll. The weight transfers backward from the ball of the left foot to the heel and is firmly on the heel through impact.

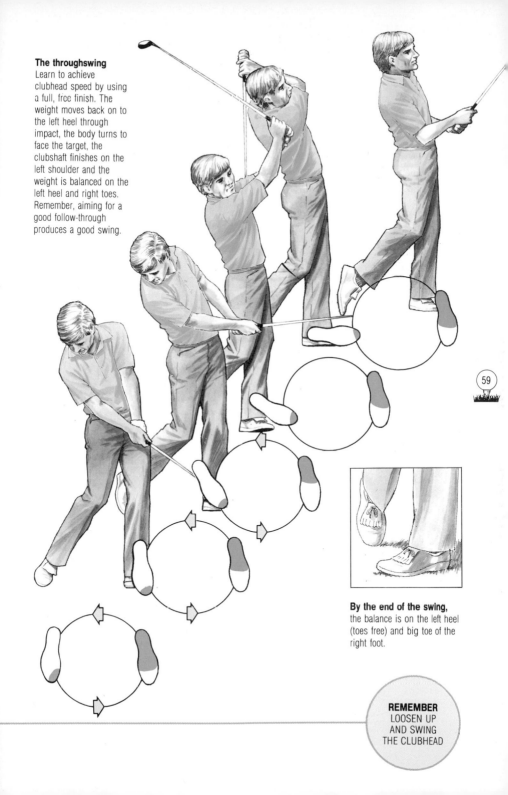

The throughswing
Learn to achieve clubhead speed by using a full, free finish. The weight moves back on to the left heel through impact, the body turns to face the target, the clubshaft finishes on the left shoulder and the weight is balanced on the left heel and right toes. Remember, aiming for a good follow-through produces a good swing.

59

By the end of the swing, the balance is on the left heel (toes free) and big toe of the right foot.

REMEMBER LOOSEN UP AND SWING THE CLUBHEAD

MORE ABOUT THE SWING

Balance is crucial to enable you to swing the clubhead at speed. Whether you have hit a good or bad shot, hold the finish for three seconds. This way your balance will improve – and so will your shots.

If you are a good player, hold the finish for three or four seconds then return the club to waist height; keep your legs still as you admire the shot to its finish!

To encourage a good strike, watch the *back* of the ball and stay looking at it until the ball has gone and you can see the ground beneath.

To add feel for direction, always align the palm of your right hand (back of the left for left-handers playing right-handed) to the clubface as though the clubface is an extension of the right arm. Learn to feel what it does. In this way the right hand will control the direction of the clubface.

The golf swing does not go straight back and through. It travels round in a circle like the swing of a squash or tennis racket. Different players swing on different planes, but all these planes are circular. As a rule shorter players tend to swing on a flatter plane than taller players.

The swing must never start back in a straight line. It must travel back on the "inside" on a curve, with the right hand then helping the club to hit out at the ball on a similar curve.

60

Balance is crucial to enable you to swing the clubhead at speed **(above)**. Hold the finish for three seconds then return the club to waist height, with your legs balanced on the left heel and tips of the right toes.

Watch the back of the ball and stay looking at it until you see the ground beneath **(left)**. At the first sign of trouble, check your concentration on the ball.

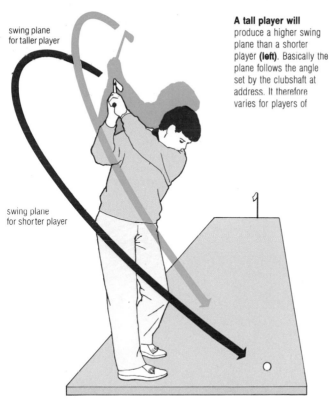

swing plane for taller player

swing plane for shorter player

A tall player will produce a higher swing plane than a shorter player **(left)**. Basically the plane follows the angle set by the clubshaft at address. It therefore varies for players of different heights and for each club through the set. The club must always move on a circular path, with backswing and throughswing mirroring each other.

In the takeaway, the club (below) moves back on a shallow curve, with shoulders turning and the clubhead moving behind the player. In a bad takeaway, the clubhead moves off plane and straight back. This leads to a bad attack, usually with long shots sliced to the right and shorter ones pulled left. Correctly, the ball is attacked from the "inside" — the right hand swinging the club out at the ball in a shallow curve, similar to the takeaway.

61

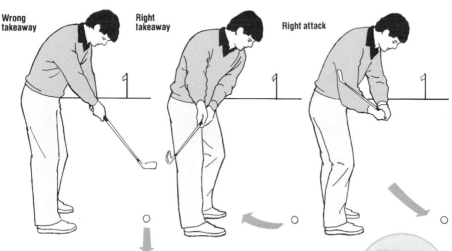

Wrong takeaway

Right takeaway

Right attack

REMEMBER
SWING THE CLUBHEAD ON A CURVE — NEVER STRAIGHT

THE SHORT IRONS

The 8, 9, 10 (pitching wedge) and the sand wedge are the short irons – with short shafts for short shots. However, the sand wedge is rarely used for full shots, although good players will use it for high shots in the range of 40 to 70 yards and adapt it for shorter pitch shots.

The 8 iron hits the farthest distance and the pitching wedge the shortest, ideally with 10 yards between clubs.

Position the ball centrally in the stance. The short shaft should bring you in close, but still stand tall. Aim for a downward attack, shifting your weight to the left foot and taking the ball and then a divot.

Let the loft of the club get the ball up. Don't try to help it up or you will fall back on your right foot and scuff the top of the ball, sending it too far. You cannot get under the ball because the ground is in the way. Hit down to force it up with a short, firm swing.

For the downward attack, the ball is played farther back in the stance. You may hit it before the swing comes round on target, and therefore push it right.

The short irons are the accuracy clubs. They are the shortest and the heaviest. The danger for beginners is failing to hit down through the ball. If they try to keep the ball up, the clubhead catches the top of the ball and sends it too low and often too far.

Trust the loft of the club. The lofts range from 43° with the 8 iron to anything from 55° to 64° with the sand iron. Hit down and the ball comes up. The distances given here are a guide for club golfers (men) to achieve. Accuracy rather than distance is the object with these clubs.

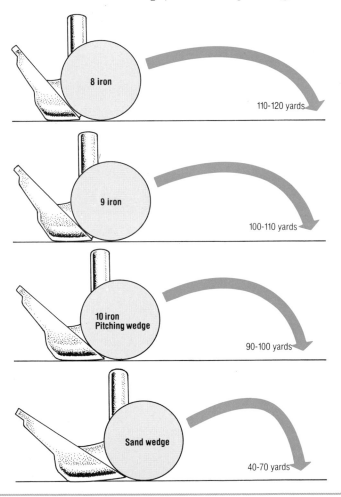

8 iron — 110-120 yards

9 iron — 100-110 yards

10 iron Pitching wedge — 90-100 yards

Sand wedge — 40-70 yards

For the beginner (left) the feeling must be of a descending contact — initially playing the ball backward of centre if necessary. Move through well on to the left foot, avoiding any tendency to try to scoop up the ball.

With the short irons (above), the swing is a little shorter and firmer, with the ball central in the stance to encourage a downward, ball then divot contact.

63

open stance

swing path

target path

CORRECTING THE STANCE
With the ball backward of centre in the stance, you may catch it before the swing is on target. If so, "open" the feet; that is, aim them left to compensate.

REMEMBER
WEIGHT LEFT.
HIT DOWN FOR
BALL AND DIVOT

LONG AND MEDIUM IRONS

The basic swing is the same for the whole set of clubs. What varies is the contact you want to achieve with each club in your armoury.

Short irons are played using a downward attack, taking the ball then a divot, whether the lie is good or bad. With long and medium irons, good players tend to vary the type of contact according to the lie.

If the ball sits well, your feet can be set with the ball slightly farther forward toward the left foot, particularly with the 3 and 4 irons. Here the ball can be swept away without any real divot.

With these longer irons, a good player is more likely to play the ball forward with a slightly upward attack when the ball sits on a good tuft of grass. For an average or tight lie, the ball needs to be played farther back for a slightly downward attack.

The ordinary golfer needs a set of clubs in which the long irons have sufficient loft to achieve good height.

The swing itself is the same from the 7 iron down to the 2 iron. You must keep the timing smooth and resist any tendency to hit too hard with the long irons.

The grip needs to be constant throughout. Take particular care with the longer irons that the extra length of shaft does not force your left hand open on the backswing.

With the long irons, remember to swing slowly and smoothly and let the club do the work. Don't force them to try to gain extra length in the shot.

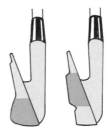

Club golfers must make sure there is enough loft on the clubs (left) and usually need the type in which weight is concentrated low in the clubhead. The type of design which keeps the ball lower is more for the professional.

Examples of the distances a male club golfer should expect from the long and medium irons, in terms of carry in still conditions:

7 iron 120–140 yards	3 iron 155–180 yards
6 iron 130–150 yards	2 iron 160–190 yards
5 iron 140–160 yards	
4 iron 150–170 yards	

7 iron

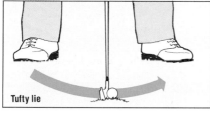

Tufty lie

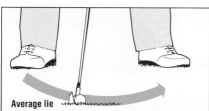

Average lie

65

From a good lie, sweep
the ball smoothly away
(right). If you have a
very good lie, collect it
slightly on the upswing
to encourage more height
and carry. The ball can
be played well forward
from a tufty lie **(above
left)**. With an average or
tight lie **(below left)**,
play it farther back for a
slightly downward attack.

6 iron 5 iron 4 iron 3 iron

REMEMBER
LONG SHAFTS
HELP LONG
SHOTS. DON'T
FORCE THEM

FAIRWAY WOODS

With the fairway woods, the swing is much the same as with the irons, although the contact from an average lie is slightly different. Here you need to sweep the ball off the grass from the bottom of the swing, rather than hitting down and through it with a divot.

The ball is played farther forward in the stance than with the irons, perhaps one third of the way from the left foot to the right foot. The width of the stance, which again must be square (parallel), remains the same as with irons.

The shaft of the woods is longer than that of the irons – again with half an inch between each number of club. This means that your posture is naturally more erect and the swing plane slightly flatter. Trust the club and it will make this happen.

Swing the clubhead on a wide, shallow path, but still round in a curve and never straight back. Do not press for distance.

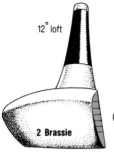

12° loft

2 Brassie

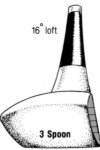

16° loft

3 Spoon

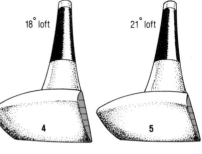

18° loft

4

21° loft

5

For good golfers and usually known as a "brassie".

Used for long shots and those requiring maximum or near maximum length. As with all woods, shafts are longer than those of irons.

For shots requiring more height and used instead of a 2 or 3 iron.

Let the length of the shaft produce clubhead speed and distance.

Turn fully in the backswing, give yourself time to change directions then swing through to a full, balanced finish.

From a good, grassy lie, simply sweep the ball, brushing away the grass on which the ball sits. Just collect the ball on the way to a full, free finish. Always rehearse the contact with a practice swing. The depth of contact is crucial.

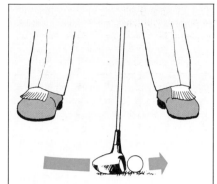

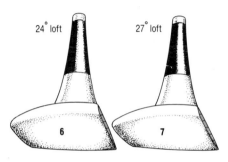

24° loft   27° loft

6   7

Suitable for the amateur instead of long irons and for semi-recovery shots from imperfect lies.

FROM A TIGHT, BARE LIE
The contact you should aim for from a tight lie with little or no grass is to bounce the club on the exact spot on which the ball sits, nipping it up and away. Bounce the sole of the club down and up, in and out like striking a match. This is a quite different contact from the ball then divot contact that is achieved with an iron.

67

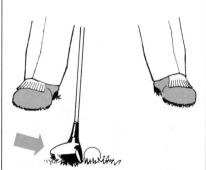

FROM A BAD LIE
Use a 4 or 5 wood from a bad lie. Aim to tip the face of the club over slightly and bring the back of the sole off the ground to get into any slight depression. Hold the shaft and hands slightly forward to the left to achieve a downward attack.

Swing the clubhead on a wide, shallow path, never straight back, and turn fully in the backswing.

REMEMBER
REHEARSE THE
DEPTH OF
CONTACT WITH
A PRACTICE
SWING

DRIVING

The driver is the longest yet lightest club in the set. You will need excellent timing to swing the clubhead through correctly, that is with the clubface square.

Because of the lack of loft, the club easily imparts sidespin to the ball. The less lofted the club, the more difficult this is likely to be. Also, faults that show with the driver often do not show at all with the 3 or 4 wood or the irons.

When driving off, you must tee the ball up correctly and at the right height. Hold the ball in the palm of your hand and perched on the tee between the first and second fingers. Press the tee into the ground with the ball, making sure that the top of the club is never below the centre of the ball. If you tee up too high, the club can go almost beneath the ball and sky it too high.

The ball should be positioned almost opposite the left heel and your feet should be wider apart than your shoulders. Make sure the right shoulder is dropped below the left; never pull it up and forward. Your right arm must hang relaxed, possibly with your hands slightly behind the ball.

At address, position the ball roughly opposite the left heel, keeping your weight central in the stance, with your right side down and relaxed.

The backswing needs to be wide and full, and you must keep your weight well behind the ball. Timing is crucial. Give yourself time for the change of direction at the top of the backswing, when the movement of the club is reversed.

The finish of the swing needs to be full and balanced, with far more weight remaining on the toes of the right foot than you would have when playing a shot with an iron.

The essentials of good driving are timing and staying behind the ball. Play the ball forward in the stance, to encourage a slight upward attack and to give maximum time to accelerate into it.

Most faults produce shots that stray off to the right. Driving is like a three-horse race from the top of the backswing – between the clubhead, the hands and the right shoulder. The clubhead has the farthest to travel, but *must always* be given time by the other two to win the race and get back to impact first.

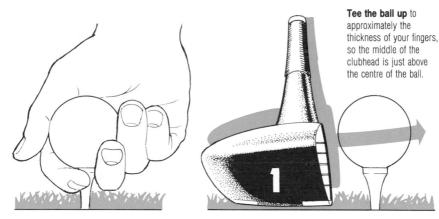

Tee the ball up to approximately the thickness of your fingers, so the middle of the clubhead is just above the centre of the ball.

69

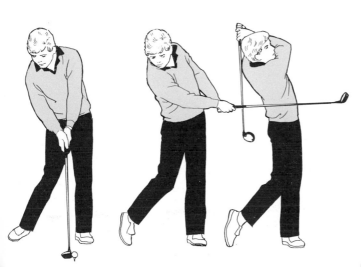

When driving, make a full turn, changing direction smoothly at the top of the backswing, then swinging through to a full, balanced finish. Keep behind the ball and sweep it away on the upswing.

REMEMBER
A DRIVER
CANNOT BE
RUSHED – IT
NEEDS TIME

MORE ABOUT DRIVING

Good driving sets you up for good scoring. The old cliché is that golfers "drive for show and putt for dough". But if you drive well, it certainly helps you improve your score.

Firstly, take care in teeing up the ball. Never simply tee up in the same spot as the player before you. Always look for a flat stance and flat lie, never a downward one. Remember that the teeing ground is the one area in which you can tread behind the ball and pick growing pieces of grass. You can also go two club-lengths behind the tee boxes. So use these rules to your advantage when teeing up.

Think, too, about alignment and position on the tee. If faced with a tee that seems to aim in the wrong direction, select the spot that gives you the most comfortable view of the fairway. Use the whole width of the tee. The view from one side may be quite different from the other. If you stand to the right of a tee, you may feel it forces you to aim left. If you set up on the left, it may make you aim right.

Look at any main trouble area from the drive and position yourself on the correct

Good driving requires sound aiming.
Always aim for a definite target, preferably something on the fairway at the distance you should hit, rather than on the far horizon. If there is not anything specific to aim at, imagine something – like a flag or bullseye.

Don't simply look at the trees or hazards to the side and try to drive between them. If you do, you are likely to be drawn toward them.

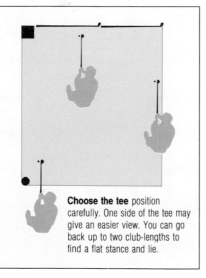

Choose the tee position carefully. One side of the tee may give an easier view. You can go back up to two club-lengths to find a flat stance and lie.

side of the tee to alleviate this. If the trouble is on the right, tee up on the right to aim away from it. Conversely, with trouble on the left, stand to the left of the tee to aim away from it.

Safety and etiquette
Accidents can happen when others who are watching stand on the wrong side of the tee, that is behind the player. Remember, the person on the tee may not be satisfied with the drive and may have another practice swing, creating danger for the person stepping forward to play next. Always be sure to walk round to the correct side of the tee before any player drives off.

REMEMBER
BE SELECTIVE
IN
TEEING UP

DRIVING STRATEGY

Good players don't simply aim to hit the ball in the middle of every fairway. They assess each hole and think before they strike. For example:

● They look for any obvious danger area off the tee.

What have the course designer and greenkeeper set as obstacles? Perhaps it is a deep bunker, a water hazard or a tree to impede the second shot.

Good players aim well away from trouble wherever possible. They choose a target on the other side of the fairway, or even in the light rough, and hit positively toward it. They make sure of avoiding trouble and may zig-zag up a hole for safety.

Club players tend to be too ambitious in trying to avoid ponds or bunkers, and aim much too close to the edge of such obstacles.

● They look for the best entrance on to the green.

The position of the bunkers or the flag may dictate that the second shot is easier from the right or the left, rather than the middle. Professionals plan for this.

● They consider the risks involved on certain tee shots and may use an iron or fairway wood instead of the driver.

This is particularly the case with bunkers at driving distance. Good players may well play short of the bunker rather than trying to skirt it, especially if the hole is short and they can still reach the green with the next shot.

They may also do this if the hole is very long, and even the risky drive well negotiated won't enable them to make the green in two.

They look at the risks involved, the depth of the bunker, and correctly assess the plusses and minuses of success or failure with the drive.

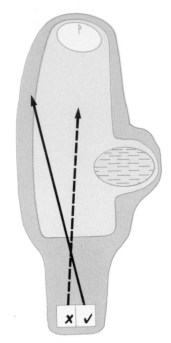

A good player will aim his shot well away from trouble and will even risk going into the light rough on the left, well away from the problem spot. The club golfer may aim away from it, but usually not far enough. A good player is prepared to zig-zag, even if this means going into the light rough. He thinks of the spot and aims positively toward it.

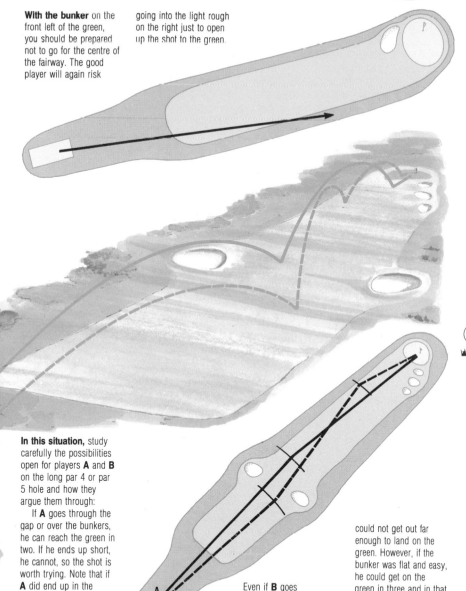

With the bunker on the front left of the green, you should be prepared not to go for the centre of the fairway. The good player will again risk going into the light rough on the right just to open up the shot to the green.

In this situation, study carefully the possibilities open for players **A** and **B** on the long par 4 or par 5 hole and how they argue them through:

If **A** goes through the gap or over the bunkers, he can reach the green in two. If he ends up short, he cannot, so the shot is worth trying. Note that if **A** did end up in the bunker, he should be able to get out and be on the green in three anyway.

Even if **B** goes through or over the obstacles, he still cannot reach the green, so the shot is not worth trying. If he did finish in a bunker, he probably could not get out far enough to land on the green. However, if the bunker was flat and easy, he could get on the green in three and in that case such an approach is worth trying.

REMEMBER
DON'T JUST
AIM DOWN
THE MIDDLE
EACH TIME

73

SHORT PUTTING: THE SET-UP

The flat-fronted grip of most putters helps you get the right kind of position – thumbs to the front, hands to the side. This is not a standard golf grip. You *don't* want the left hand on the top, with the right beneath; you want the palms facing.

Most professionals use the reverse overlap grip, with the pads of the thumbs down the front of the club and the left index finger outside the last two fingers of the right hand. The left index finger then controls and steadies the backswing.

A popular grip used by amateurs is to put the right index finger down the back of the shaft in addition to, or instead of, the reverse overlap. The index fingers steady the length of the stroke and provide feel, direction and distance.

At address you should ideally carry your left wrist in a high position – arched up, not dropped down as for the long game. This position is made easier with the upright lie of the putter. Spread your elbows and tuck them backward into your body. Alternatively, though this is usually more difficult, allow the arms to hang straight. Either way, your left wrist should ride high.

Your eyes should be directly over the ball and parallel to the line of the putt, with your head horizontal so that it swivels to look along the line. If, wrongly, you hold your head high, it will turn and lift instead of rotating.

Putting stances vary enormously. In practice, the line along the feet and shoulders can be at virtually any angle – as long as it works. As a starting point, a stance with the line across the toes and shoulders parallel to the putt is easiest, with the ball positioned fairly centrally and your weight opposite the ball.

74

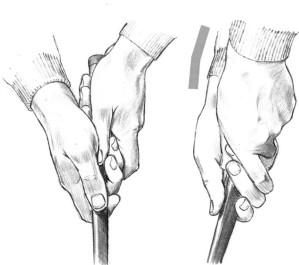

The reverse overlap grip – thumbs to the front, palms to the side and the left index finger outside the right-hand fingers.

Another view of the reverse overlap grip, with wrists arched up, not dropped.

The addition of the right index finger down the shaft can add control to the stroke.

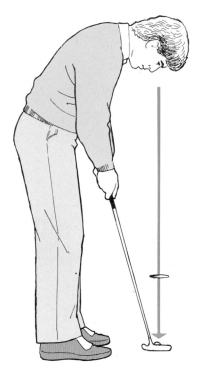

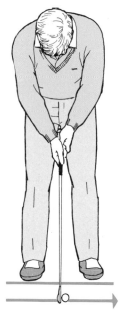

Aim to have your eyes directly over the ball **(left)** and parallel to the putt.

Start with your weight fairly evenly on the feet, with the ball central or just ahead of centre.

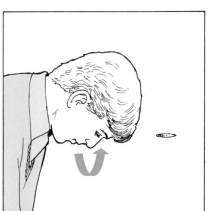

Although you must stand well up and not crouch, your head should be in a horizontal position **(above)**. From here it swivels to see the line of the putt. If the head is too high, it tends to turn and lift rather than swivel **(above right)**, usually resulting in problems with direction.

REMEMBER
HIGH ARCHED
WRISTS –
NEVER LOW
OR DROPPED

AIMING THE SHORT PUTTS

When short putting, many errors arise simply from poor aiming. It is essential that the clubface is directed at the target and that the club sits flat on the ground, *not* toe up. A putter with a broad back and a line – or series of lines – on it is usually the easiest to aim.

The line can be aimed on target more

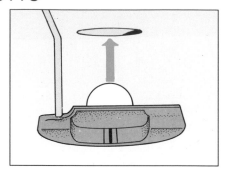

A putter with a line (or several) on the top of the head is often easier to line up correctly. Aim the line rather than the face. Check it from behind, if necessary.

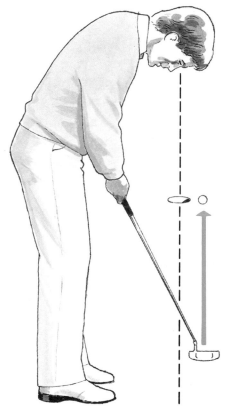

Your eyes should, in theory, be directly over the ball and parallel to the putt. If they are "outside" the ball, the tendency is to pull the putt to the left.

With your eyes "inside" the line of the ball, you are likely to push the putt to the right.

easily by setting the face accurately. Hold it in position and check from behind.

Check the following points:
● Your eyes are over the ball. If they are outside the ball, you may well aim left.
● You can see the line of the shot. To test this put the ball 6 feet from the hole and place a small coin directly on line 18 inches ahead of the ball. Judge this line from behind the ball. At address, do the three look in line? If so, you are lucky. If not, you have visual distortion. This can

be corrected by a trip to the opticians, by using trial and error to move your head position, or by practising until the three all appear on line.

The practice swing for a short putt is vital. When you do one, do not aim it at the hole. If you do, you need to address the ball and change the angle. This is one of the most common reasons for aiming right. Instead, either aim the practice swing parallel to the putt or carry it out in a completely random direction.

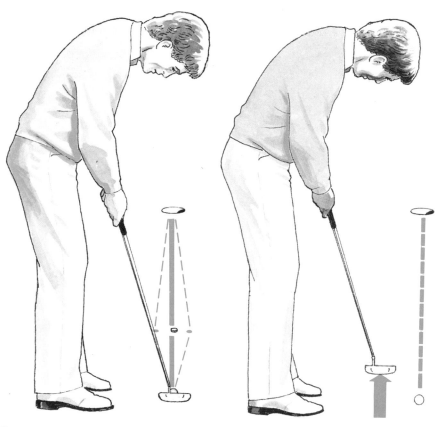

77

Line up the ball, a coin and the hole from behind. Do they appear in a straight line as you

address the putt? If not, try adjusting your head position.

Never do the practice swing *at* the hole — always parallel to the putt.

REMEMBER
PRACTISE YOUR
SWING PARALLEL
TO THE HOLE
NEVER AT IT

THE SHORT PUTTING STROKE

Always swing the putter just above the ground – never brush the grass. Concentrate on striking the very back of the ball. For short putts of up to 6 feet, you must get the feel that the putter moves back and through in a perfectly straight line, although in reality it may travel on a slight curve.

As you address the ball, tuck in the right elbow. This should keep the putter moving back just enough inside the line. Swing the putter slowly back and through, letting it rise and fall quite naturally. Backswing and throughswing should be roughly equal in length.

Ideally the putter head should move straight through to the hole, without being pulled back on an inside curve. If you use a putter with a line on the top, feel that you are swinging that line straight through to the hole.

Some players stroke putts slowly and smoothly; others tap them in. With good fast greens a slow, smooth stroke is ideal. On rough or winter greens, a firm tap can be more effective.

In either instance, finish the stroke with the clubhead in a stationary position and your head perfectly still. More short putts are spoilt by looking up early than for any other reason. Keep your head and eyes still and watch the ball from the corner of your left eye or, ideally, listen for it to drop.

This helps you to keep the shoulders rocking back and through on line and in turn to maintain a good path for the putting stroke.

Develop a routine for short putting. Set the clubface squarely; position your feet; check the aim; lift the putter to check you are supporting it rather than resting it on the ground; reset it; then swing slowly and smoothly, with head and eyes still.

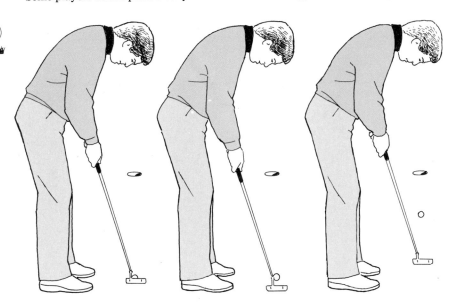

For short putts of, say, up to 8 feet, be sure to *feel* the putter moving in a straight path. In reality, it comes back on a slight curve, then straight through to the hole. Keep your head perfectly still and listen for the ball to drop. Do not be tempted to look up at the ball before this.

PLAY

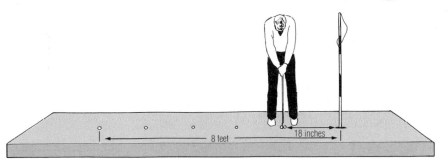

Practise short putting (above) by setting up balls from 18 inches to 8 feet from the hole. Start with the closest and work through the line. If you miss one, start again. It adds a little competitive edge to your practice.

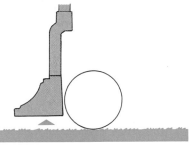

The putter should always hang from your arms and shoulders before you make the stroke **(left)**. Never rest the putter on the ground at address or you risk lifting it up and jerking it away in the backswing. Always swing the putter above the ground.

79

Swing the putter at a consistent level above the ground, fairly low in the backswing and then through and up toward the hole. Never brush the ground. Keep the putter above it for a clean, consistent strike.

REMEMBER
LIFT AND RESET PUTTER FOR A SLOW, SMOOTH STROKE

SHORT AND MEDIUM PUTTING

Short putting, that is up to 6 feet, is mainly a question of direction, reading the putt well, aiming correctly and having a perfect stroke. But in certain situations the right speed is also vital.

A short putt on a sloping green has to have the correct combination of line and length. For each putt you need to allow for the break to the right or left, while at the same time considering how firmly you want to strike the ball.

The more firmly the ball is struck, the better it holds the line and the less borrow you need to allow. If you aim to trickle the ball in slowly, it is going to move far more off line.

You have two choices – to hit the ball boldly and straight, or to hit it cautiously, allowing for the curve. Practise both. Do exactly the same in practice as you would on the course.

A putt must be struck firmly enough to

Always aim for a putt to finish a foot past the hole in case it misses. This way it holds its line to the hole. If you do miss, the return is a formality.

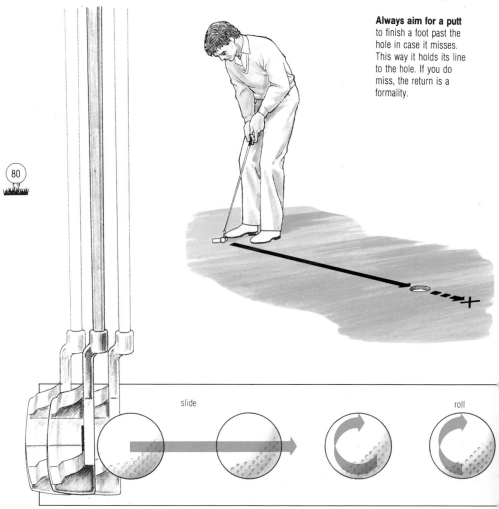

slide

roll

hold its line. Distance is particularly
crucial for medium length putts of, say, 8
to 12 feet. You need to hit the ball firmly
enough to keep it rolling smoothly but
without going too far past if you do miss
the hole.

Players often feel a putt is unlucky
when it moves off line just by the hole.
They blame the cut and condition of the
green. Usually the ball has simply not
been hit firmly enough. In the last 3 or 4
inches it can turn almost at right angles,
even on a perfect green. It will take up
any slight imperfections or undulations
in the green.

The ball slides for a moment as it
leaves the putter, then rolls and, when
slowing down, wobbles. If you miss the
putt, this may simply be because you
have underhit it. The ball must be
running fast enough to drop into the hole
before it wobbles.

Distance is crucial. Aim for a length in
which, if the ball does miss, it will run
about a foot past the hole.

A short putt on a slope
can be approached as a
firm, straight shot or as a
more cautious putt with a
substantial break.

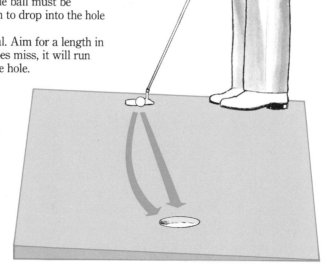

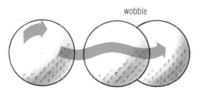

wobble

A ball slides, then
rolls and finally
wobbles in the last few
inches. Hit it firmly
enough to get it in the
hole before it wobbles.

REMEMBER
A FIRM
PUTT HOLDS
ITS LINE

LONG PUTTING

Good long putting depends on excellent judgement of distance. It is easy to be several yards short of or past the flag, while unlikely that you will make as much error with direction.

The stroke itself becomes less important than with short putting. Allow your hands and wrists to come into play to get a feel for the length. A long putt of the right strength is usually fairly successful. Aim at making every long putt pass the hole by 6 inches to 2 feet.

Remember that the putter should never brush the ground. Focus your attention on the back of the ball and keep the swing as slow and smooth as possible.

To judge the line, look for the overall slope of the green and assess whether you are going across it. Aim to the side, if necessary, to allow for this.

If the break is small, choose a spot to the side of the hole and roll the ball to this. If the break is large and the green fast, choose a spot, say, two-thirds of the way and off to the side and try to roll the ball out over this. Always think of the putt as a straight putt to the spot you have chosen.

When having the flag attended, ask your caddy to stand to the higher side of the hole. This can help you to aim to the side you want.

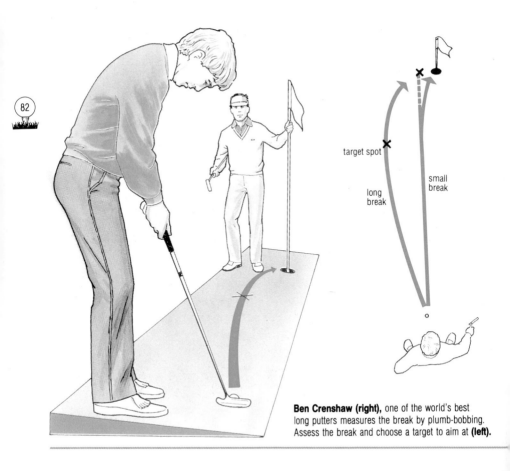

target spot

long break

small break

Ben Crenshaw (right), one of the world's best long putters measures the break by plumb-bobbing. Assess the break and choose a target to aim at **(left).**

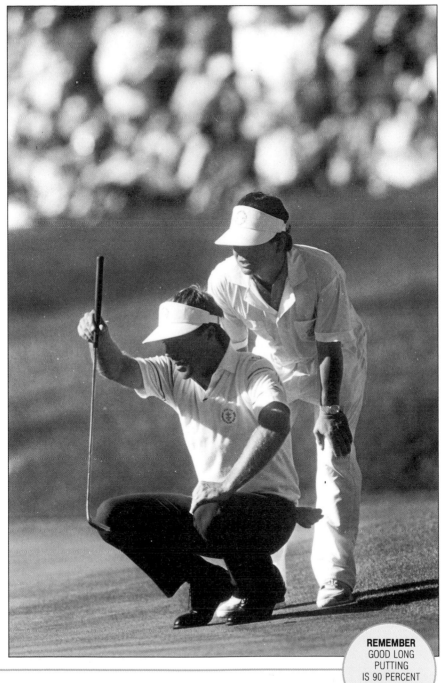

83

REMEMBER
GOOD LONG
PUTTING
IS 90 PERCENT
JUDGEMENT OF
DISTANCE

READING GREENS

When approaching the green, look for the overall slope and remember that the back is usually higher than the front. If the green looks flat – BEWARE! It probably slopes down to the back.

The slope shows most when you look up at it, so find the lowest point of the green and look from there to see the overall slope. Go behind the putt to judge the side slope and always look quickly from the side to assess the uphill or downhill slope. A downhill putt can often be misleading and appears flat. You are looking over the slope and tend to underestimate it.

Remember, too, that the wind can affect putts, particularly if you are putting downhill, fast and downwind.

Think distance all the time. You can go 8 feet past, but you are most unlikely to be 8 feet to the side.

Reading the green for a long putt can be done quickly. Do it while you are approaching the green, taking your clubs round to be ready for your shot, or while your partners are putting. Assess the overall slope rather than being over concerned about any irregularity en route.

Experience of your own course will alert you to any oddities with certain

Beware the green with an adjacent large tree **(above)**. If to the south, it may leave the green in shadow all day, making it slow. Look, too, for large roots which will drain off moisture; these can make the green both bumpy and fast.

**Expect a plateau green
(left)** to drain well and be
fast. A green in a basin
(below), by contrast,
may gather moisture and
be slow.

greens. But how do good putters learn to
read an unfamiliar green accurately first
time? The following are examples of what
you should look out for:

● Overhanging trees can leave a green in
shade all day. Look for a slow green.
However, the roots can draw moisture and
create a quick, bare green.

● Plateau greens often drain fast and
play quick. Basin greens can hold
moisture and play slow.

● Good players study the growth of the
grass and the moisture. Some greens can
get noticeably slower as dusk gathers,
since the grass grows a little during the
day and holds moisture.

● Look for the grain – the general
direction in which the grass grows. Early
in the day, look at the mower lines. On the
dark strips, the grass is lying toward you

and is slow; on the pale ones, it lies away
from you and is faster.

● In most climates there is noticeable
grain on the green, since the grass grows
in a specific direction. Allow for this in
just the same way as on a slope – fast
with the grain, slow against it. Across the
grain the ball will be pushed off line, often
quite dramatically.

(85)

WATCHING THE GRASS GROW
When reading greens, look for the following
grass characteristics:

● Growing toward the sea.
● Growing toward the setting sun.
● Growing in the direction golfers walk.
● Growing away from mountain tops.
● Growing with the direction of the water
supply.

**Look at the overall
slope** of the green **(left)**
as you approach it.
Assume all putts will
follow this overall slope
unless you can clearly
see evidence to the
contrary.

REMEMBER
JUDGE THE
LINE FROM
THE OVERALL
SLOPE

READING GREENS FOR SHORT PUTTS

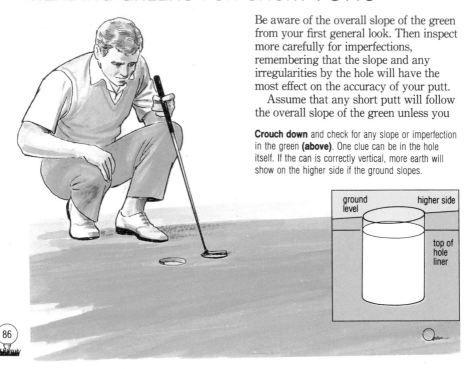

Be aware of the overall slope of the green from your first general look. Then inspect more carefully for imperfections, remembering that the slope and any irregularities by the hole will have the most effect on the accuracy of your putt.

Assume that any short putt will follow the overall slope of the green unless you

Crouch down and check for any slope or imperfection in the green **(above)**. One clue can be in the hole itself. If the can is correctly vertical, more earth will show on the higher side if the ground slopes.

ground level   higher side

top of hole liner

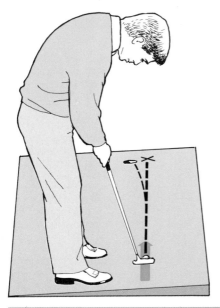

Whatever point you choose to aim for, always play a straight putt **(left)**. Don't be tempted with a right-to-left putt, for example, to move your putter in a curved path **(below)**. Always play straight back and through.

can clearly see a reason why it should not.

If there is a slope on the green, you have to decide whether to be bold or cautious with the breaking putt. On a fast green, either hit firmly and straight or allow for the slope and trickle the ball more slowly. Whichever approach you prefer, choose a definite spot to aim at and play a straight putt to that point with your usual routine.

Never lose the straight back and through feeling or the stroke will become a curve. With a left-to-right putt in particular, your feet are below the ball and it is easy to produce a curved path and lose the straight one.

With a left-to-right putt, a useful technique is to play the ball toward the heel of the club. This will help to hold it up to the left.

PLUMB-BOBBING
Some players use the plumb-bobbing method for judging a slope on the green. Broadly speaking, you stand out from the slope with your feet fairly wide apart.

Hang your putter in front of you with your thumb and forefinger. From directly behind the ball, look at the hole with your master eye, shutting the other, and line up the putter shaft against, say, the left side of the ball.

If the hole also appears against the putter shaft, there is probably little or no slope. If the hole is to the right of the shaft, the odds are you have a left-to-right slope, and a right-to-left one if to the left.

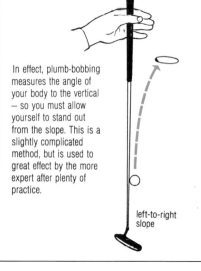

In effect, plumb-bobbing measures the angle of your body to the vertical – so you must allow yourself to stand out from the slope. This is a slightly complicated method, but is used to great effect by the more expert after plenty of practice.

left-to-right slope

87

Whether you choose a straight, firm putt or a softer one allowing for the slope, always aim and play straight to a definite aiming point.

REMEMBER
EVERY PUTT
IS STRAIGHT
TO YOUR
AIM POINT

PRACTISING SHORT PUTTS

When playing a short putt, you should always move your putter straight back and through. You can move it fractionally inside on the backswing, but never move it outside.

One way of checking that your putter is moving through in a straight line is to practise swinging along another club-shaft, keeping the backswing on line. If your problem is pulling the putter off line when going through the shot, practise between two clubs laid parallel on the ground.

To check that you are striking the ball on the "sweet spot" of the putter, stick a piece of paper on the face and practise hitting accurately from this spot until you get it right.

Your swing should carry on through in the direction of the hole, with the putter naturally rising slightly. Develop this by rolling and pushing the ball to the hole from 18 inches – no more – and with no backswing. This stroke is actually

illegal, so you should only use it as a technique for practice.

When practising your short putting, work from 3 to 4 feet. You should achieve 100 percent success. An error in the putt from this distance is your fault and not that of the green. Put a little pressure on yourself.

See how many consecutive 4-foot putts you can hole, and keep on practising until you really are perfect.

Another good exercise is to place six balls in a circle around the hole and try to putt each one in turn. This is particularly useful for tackling varying sidehill putts.

Work on developing a bold approach to short putting by sticking a tee or ball marker in the back of the hole and trying to strike it with the ball every time. To make the hole look a bigger and easier target in actual play, practise with the sides blocked off with tees. Then the ball can only go in the middle of the hole.

Place two clubs on the ground parallel to the line of your putt to check that you are swinging your putter through in a straight line.

Mark the "sweet spot" on the putter face with a piece of paper and try hitting the ball each time on this spot.

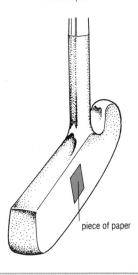

piece of paper

This is good short putting practice. Place six balls in a circle around the hole at a distance of 4 feet and try putting each in turn. Remember, the more you practise the better your putting will become.

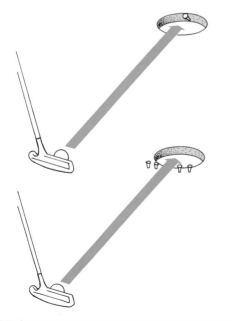

PUSH STROKE PRACTICE
Although this shot is illegal in play, it is a good way of developing a straight swing and follow-through. Play it from about 18 inches with no backswing and keep the putter on line through the push.

Two ways of aiming for the centre of the hole are to put a tee in the back of the hole **(above left)** and block off either side of the hole with tees **(left)**.

These practice strategies will help your accuracy and your confidence on the course.

REMEMBER
GOOD SHORT
PUTTING
BOOSTS LONG
PUTTING

PRACTISING LONG PUTTS

Short putting requires a good stroke. Long putting is more a question of feel for length and slope. Practise judging distances and work at getting it right first time. Any fool can do it correctly a second or third time.

A simple way to practise long putting is to work around the practice putting green, holing out every short one. To combine long and short putting, play the professional's game of "lay backs". If you leave a tap-in, always move it back a putter's length. This forces you to hole from 3 to 5 feet every time you miss!

If you have a green to yourself, try setting down two pieces of string, say 6 feet apart, and work for length at finishing between them. As you improve, make the target area narrower, concentrating all the time on distance more than direction. This can be adapted for indoor practice with shorter, medium-length putts.

On the course, but without holding up play, put the ball to the edge of the green after completing the hole.

90

To concentrate on length rather than direction, putt the ball back to the edge of the green after completing each hole **(below)**. Be sure not to hold up play while you do this.

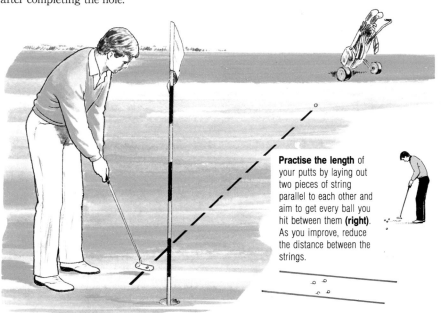

Practise the length of your putts by laying out two pieces of string parallel to each other and aim to get every ball you hit between them **(right)**. As you improve, reduce the distance between the strings.

To check your long putting stroke and feel, use four balls. Aim at a target and strike the first ball. Without looking up, now strike the second, then the third and finally the fourth. If your striking is good, all four should finish close together.

Use different numbers or colours of the same make of ball and you may begin to feel errors in the stroke. The depth may be inconsistent, perhaps because you are snagging the ground occasionally or striking the ball too high.

Check your aiming. Have someone attend the flag on a long putt, nominate your line and ask him to check whether you are starting the ball where you intend. Many players nominate a line, allowing insufficient to the side, and then subconsciously try to correct this. Be accurate for every putt.

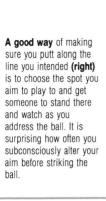

On the practice putting green, if you miss a long putt but only just **(above)**, instead of tapping in, move the ball back the length of your putter and play it from there. These "lay backs" of 3 to 5 feet will quickly make you try harder with the first putt.

91

A good way of making sure you putt along the line you intended **(right)** is to choose the spot you aim to play to and get someone to stand there and watch as you address the ball. It is surprising how often you subconsciously alter your aim before striking the ball.

REMEMBER
NEVER BRUSH
THE GROUND
WHEN PUTTING

CHIPPING AND RUNNING: 1

When playing chipping and running shots around the green, aim to get the ball down on the ground as early as possible.

Using a putter

When possible, use your putter around the green on bare or smooth ground. Remember you are only trying to hit the back of the ball. You do not brush the ground. This means that the putter is particularly useful from certain poor lies such as sandy soil, loose leaves or muddy ground. If you try to pitch from a poor lie, good contact can be difficult. With a putter, it is easier.

You can also use a putter to play from small depressions or holes around the green. The ball will not run smoothly, and may start with a hop, but the stroke can still be far easier than a chip.

The putter should also be used for playing up and down banks where the ground is bare, even if it is not absolutely smooth. If you cannot putt the ball, the next choice is to run it with a 6 or 7 iron. Ideally make this stroke as close as possible to a putt.

Judging distances

With chipping, your approach should be much the same as for putting. If the ground is bare, the ball need not necessarily be landed right on the green. You can judge the stroke by thinking of the overall length rather than where the ball lands.

If the grass is at all rough and you cannot run the ball through it, you need to be aware of where the ball is going to land. In this case, if the flag is close to the near edge of the green, the 6 or 7 iron may no longer be suitable.

You need to alter the ratio of carry to run and think of the landing spot. A more lofted club, such as the 9 iron or pitching wedge, will give you less run in relation to carry. Errors with these more lofted clubs can, however, be more disastrous, so stick to running shots where you can.

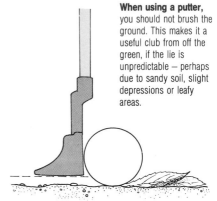

When using a putter, you should not brush the ground. This makes it a useful club from off the green, if the lie is unpredictable – perhaps due to sandy soil, slight depressions or leafy areas.

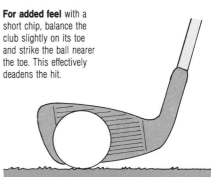

For added feel with a short chip, balance the club slightly on its toe and strike the ball nearer the toe. This effectively deadens the hit.

This is incorrect. The clubhead must never pass the hands in an attempt to scoop the ball up. Keep the wrists arched and firm.

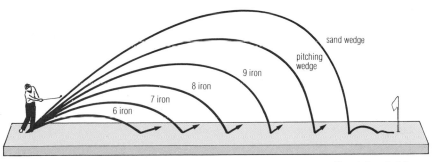

sand wedge

pitching wedge

9 iron

8 iron

7 iron

6 iron

The choice of club depends on the ratio of carry to loft **(above)**. The less lofted the club, the safer the shot.

The choice of club (right) is important. Preferably use a putter, since there is little that can go wrong when using this club.

If a putter is unsuitable, the next choice **(below)** is a 6 or 7 iron. Play a running shot and judge it in terms of overall length.

93

Look to pitch the ball (below) only if you cannot use a putter or decide a running shot is unsuitable.

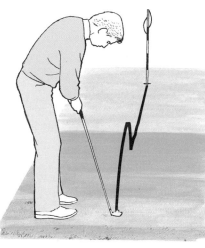

REMEMBER CHOOSE IN ORDER: PUTT, RUN, PITCH

CHIPPING AND RUNNING: 2

When playing the chip shot, many professionals use the reverse overlap grip, and certainly most play the shot with their thumbs more to the front of the grip, rather than having the left hand over, as in the standard Vardon grip.

Good chippers stand close to the ball. For the shorter player, this often means having the club more upright than normal and balanced slightly toward the toe.

To get the right feel for your chipping stroke, first set up with your putter and, with much the same stance and grip, take hold of your 6 or 7 iron. Gripping the club

The chipping stroke – back and through the same length, very similar to a putting stroke. Start with the elbows in, wrists up and weight favouring the left foot. You should just brush the ground on which the ball is sitting **(below)**.

like a putter, arch the left wrist up so your hands and arms swing the club back and through without any wrist action. You should feel quite stiff-wristed when playing the short chip, unless you are a very advanced player.

Play the shot with the ball central in the stance, with your hands and weight slightly ahead of the ball, and swing the club back and through with a neat stroke, just brushing the ground on which the ball sits. To gain greater feel, flex your knees slightly, turn both feet a little toward the target and keep your hands and wrists up and forward.

With very short chip shots, play the ball more toward the toe of the club than for long shots. This gives you a softer feel and more delicate control over the stroke.

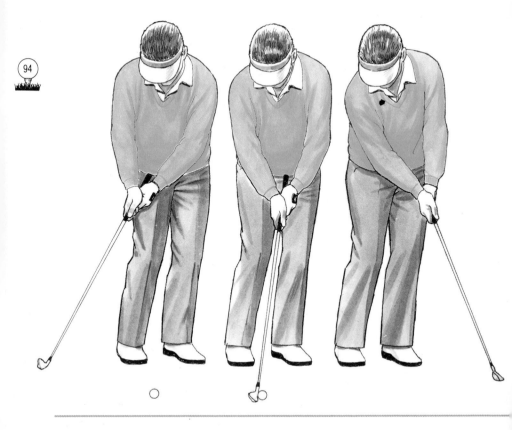

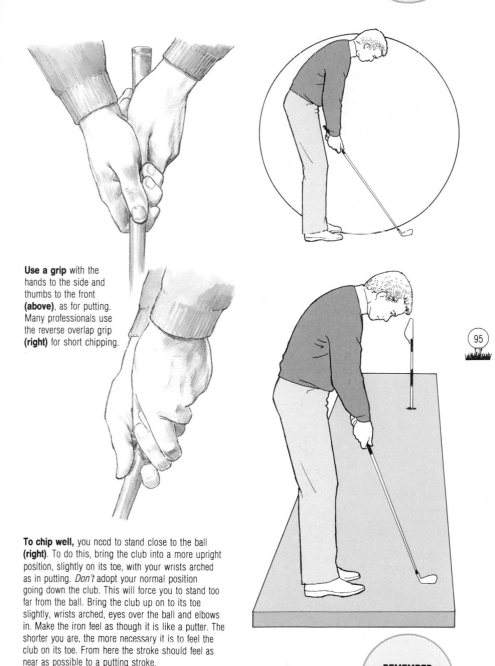

95

Use a grip with the
hands to the side and
thumbs to the front
(above), as for putting.
Many professionals use
the reverse overlap grip
(right) for short chipping.

To chip well, you nccd to stand close to the ball
(right). To do this, bring the club into a more upright
position, slightly on its toe, with your wrists arched
as in putting. *Don't* adopt your normal position
going down the club. This will force you to stand too
far from the ball. Bring the club up on to its toe
slightly, wrists arched, eyes over the ball and elbows
in. Make the iron feel as though it is like a putter. The
shorter you are, the more necessary it is to feel the
club on its toe. From here the stroke should feel as
near as possible to a putting stroke.

REMEMBER
CHIP AS
YOU PUTT

LONG PITCHING

Once you get within a full 9-iron distance of the green, you will need to play a pitch shot. The long pitch is used from about 45 to 100 yards. You can play longer pitch shots with a pitching wedge or 9 iron and the shorter ones with a pitching or sand wedge. The sand wedge can be useful from about 50 yards or closer.

Set up with the ball central in the stance, your hands ahead of the ball and your weight more on the left foot. With the wrists down and forward, you have a ready-made "wrist cock".

Hold the club firmly with the left hand, increase the wrist cock very slightly in the backswing, then transfer your weight well on to the left foot in the downswing, using a downward attack – ball then divot – with a short, firm finish.

The stance is important here. The ball must be back in the stance and your hands forward to ensure a downward attack. By having the ball nearer your right foot, there is a tendency to hit out to the right.

By trial and error, find out how much you need to turn your feet toward the target for the ball to fly straight. Turn the left foot round and the right foot in. This

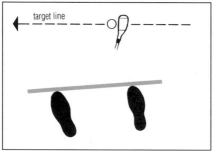

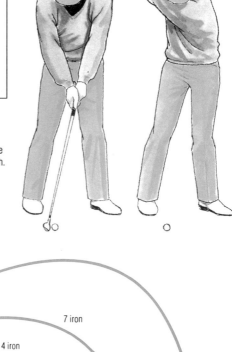

With long pitching and punch shots **(above)**, play the ball back in the stance. Turn the line of the feet left until this brings the shot on target.

With the long pitch (right), limit the backswing to allow you to accelerate through the ball to a controlled finish. Never flick or loosen your wrist in the throughswing.

The long pitch can be adapted using a 4 or 7 iron **(below)** to produce lower punched shots, using the same technique. A running shot is often safer for the high handicap player and necessary in the wind.

7 iron

4 iron

right foot position is important. Also, make the stance fairly wide to allow you to transfer your weight on to the left foot.

With shorter shots, reduce the backswing slightly and slow down the throughswing, but be sure to accelerate the club through impact.

The normal fault of the high handicap player is in trying to scoop the ball up and into the air. In practice, try to keep your head still and avoid looking up to see where the ball goes.

A good practice routine is to set out various targets – an umbrella, golf bag or ball bag – at different distances from 50 to 90 yards and work at landing the ball as close to these as possible.

Good players can hit long pitch shots with either a draw, that is slightly right to left, or a fade, slightly left to right. The draw pitch is good for keeping the ball moving forward, particularly on a long green or into the wind. You can play this by holding the face of the club closed and attacking the ball from the inside.

The faded pitch, with a little cut spin, is used for stopping the ball quickly on the green. You play it by opening the face slightly at address and holding it open through impact.

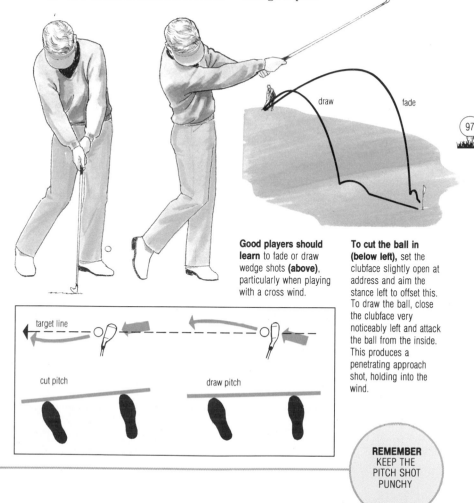

97

Good players should learn to fade or draw wedge shots **(above)**, particularly when playing with a cross wind.

target line

cut pitch

draw pitch

To cut the ball in (below left), set the clubface slightly open at address and aim the stance left to offset this. To draw the ball, close the clubface very noticeably left and attack the ball from the inside. This produces a penetrating approach shot, holding into the wind.

REMEMBER
KEEP THE
PITCH SHOT
PUNCHY

SHORT PITCHING

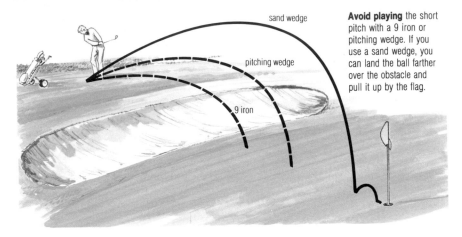

sand wedge

pitching wedge

9 iron

Avoid playing the short pitch with a 9 iron or pitching wedge. If you use a sand wedge, you can land the ball farther over the obstacle and pull it up by the flag.

The nightmare for many club golfers is the little shot over a bunker with the flag no more than 20 yards away. The best club to use here is the sand wedge, since it allows you to carry the ball farther over the obstacle and make it pull up quickly. Although it is the heaviest in the bag, don't be afraid of it.

The sand and pitching wedges are constructed differently. The pitching wedge has a sharp leading edge and can easily dig into the ground. In fact, it is designed to take a divot. The sand wedge has a slightly raised leading edge and a rounded flange and is designed to bounce on the ground. Most pros use it far more around the green than a pitching wedge.

To play the short pitch shot, set up with your normal grip, checking that your hands are to the side of the club. Do not let the left hand go too far over or the right hand too far under. Firm up the wrists and grip the club as tightly as possible with the left hand.

Imagine that your arms are tied to your body so that you have to make a firm-wristed swing with plenty of leg action. Cut out any wrist action.

To prepare for the shot, have two practice swings and bounce the club on the ground. Don't just tickle the grass; feel

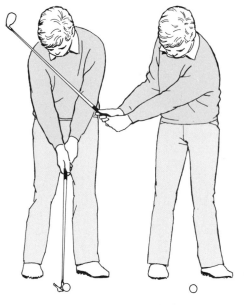

the flange making contact with the ground. This will allow you to judge the depth of the swing accurately.

Set up to the ball, look once at your landing spot, then concentrate on the firm-wristed swing, back and through, brushing the ground, and listen for the ball to land on the green.

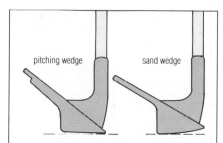

pitching wedge   sand wedge

The sand wedge has more loft than the pitching wedge and is made to bounce rather than cut in. With the short pitch, you don't want a divot. Just hold the club down through impact and feel the flange dent the ground.

The short pitch is a shot in which you use your ears rather than your eyes. Listen for the practice swing to brush the ground and listen for the ball to land at the other end. Resist the urge to follow the ball with your eyes. Look at the ball only after you have heard it land.

This shot is used for short distances around the green. The more grass the ball sits on, the easier the short pitch is to play. Practise first from grassy lies, then adapt the method for more difficult shots from less grassy or bare lies. Never be tempted to use wrist action unless you want a shot of at least 25 yards or if the ball is sitting in a slight hole.

The short pitch shot (left) is played with wrists firm and elbows as though tied into the body. Move back and through with your shoulders and legs, making sure the backswing and throughswing are the same length. Keep the clubface looking up beyond impact.

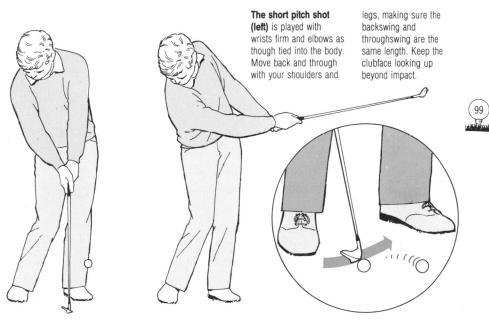

99

Playing this shot is all about keeping your head still and judging the depth properly. The loft of the club will get the ball up for you. If you purposely try to lift the ball, the clubhead will rise and catch the top of it. Simply work at holding the club down to the ground and at getting the bottom of the ball.

Never try to lift the ball when playing a short pitch shot. The club will catch the top of the ball **(above)** and top it. Make a U-shaped swing, brushing the ground beneath the ball. Think "down" in order to get the ball up.

REMEMBER
LISTEN FOR
THE BALL
TO LAND

THE CUT SHOT

The cut shot is used for extra height – getting up and over a bush or high bank, for example. When playing a short cut shot around the green, use the sand wedge and open the clubface to provide you with extra loft.

First set up with the clubface square, with the bottom groove of the face pointing directly out in front of you. Then loosen your grip, rotate the top of the shaft until the clubface turns about 10 degrees, and grip the club again.

To play the cut shot, turn your feet and the club until the face is aimed at the target. Use a fairly full swing, keeping your left wrist firm through impact and holding the clubface open as it slides beneath the ball. The best way to learn this shot is to practise teeing up the ball on a tuft of grass, with the feeling of sliding the clubface under it.

If you watch good players using this shot you will notice that the left wrist leads in an upward position through impact, which keeps the clubface open and upward.

The shot itself is used fairly infrequently, but it is important for developing your bunker shots.

OPENING THE CLUBFACE

There are three points you must remember about the open clubface:

1 Keep the ball up toward the toe of the club, never the socket.

2 Although it may look awkward, the more rounded the face of your club, the easier it will seem.

3 The grip on the club is not round but egg-shaped. When you open the face, the point of the egg shape is in a different part of your hands and the grip may therefore feel uncomfortable. Open the clubface first, then grip it.

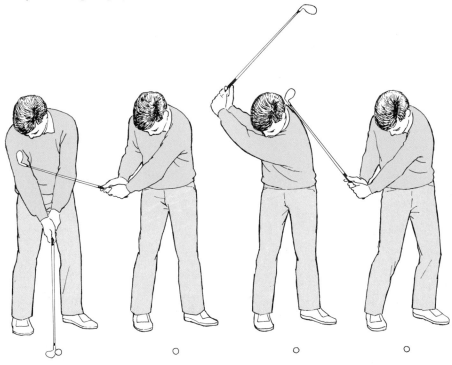

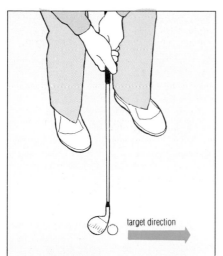

Open the clubface about 10 degrees, then turn your feet around to the left until the clubface is aiming on target.

target direction

Practise a cut shot by teeing the ball well up on tufty grass. Lay the clubface on its back and get the feeling that you are holding it open. Then try to slide it beneath the ball.

101

Play the cut shot with a sand wedge, keeping the ball forward in the stance and the clubface open. Make a full slow swing, holding the face open and sliding it beneath the ball. Let the left elbow draw back behind you beyond impact in order to maintain this open-faced action.

REMEMBER
OPEN THE
CLUBFACE
FIRST, THEN
GRIP IT

BUNKER SHOTS: THE RIGHT WEAPON

Club golfers usually find bunker shots difficult because they have problems with their equipment. A good sand wedge is one of the most important clubs in the set, but remember that it is quite different from a pitching wedge.

Not only does the sand wedge have more loft, but the leading edge is rounded as you look down at it and it is also blunt. A good sand wedge also has a slightly rounded flange, so that the lowest part of the clubhead is the back of the flange.

A pitching wedge is designed to cut through turf and has a sharp leading edge, which is the lowest part of the clubhead. This will often cut into sand in the bunker and get stuck.

Ideally a sand wedge should have plenty of loft and many professionals use one with at least 60 degrees. Club manufacturers often make sand wedges with insufficient loft. This means you have to open the clubface, which can complicate the shot.

The lie of the sand wedge is also important. If you work up through a set of clubs, the higher the numbers, the more upright they become. In other words, the 3 irons sits fairly low, while the pitching wedge will sit up. Most professionals use the sand wedge, which has the lie of a pitching wedge, or a 9 iron.

Play the bunker shot with your hands

low, knees flexed and, if anything, sink a little into the sand. As well as insufficient loft, manufacturers often make the lie of the sand wedge too upright. With less loft, you have to open the clubface more; and this can be even more awkward for the golfer if the lie is too upright.

If you do have difficulty opening the clubface, you may also find that a perfectly round grip can make this easier. So, too, does a round shape to the head. With these, the club looks less awkward when it is sitting open.

Check the lie of your sand wedge. Preferably this should be flatter than the pitching wedge. If you have difficulty in opening the clubface, try a club with a perfectly rounded grip.

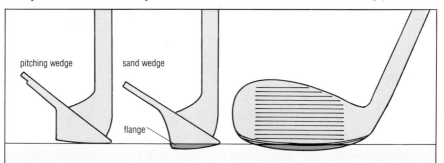

pitching wedge

sand wedge

flange

The lowest point on a pitching wedge is the leading edge; on a sand wedge it is the flange. Any sand wedge without a proper flange cuts and digs into the sand instead of bouncing through. Look, too, for a club with 60 degrees of loft and a rounded edge to help you open the clubface more easily.

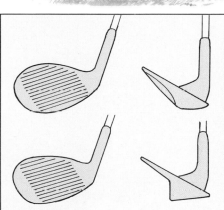

When playing in exceptionally soft or heavy sand, experiment with sand wedges with varying flanges — both rounded **(above)** and flat **(below)**. For preference, go for a "middle of the road" sand wedge that is useful for pitching and sand shots around the green.

When using a sand wedge in a bunker **(above)**, keep your hands low, flex your knees slightly and sink your feet a little into the sand.

REMEMBER
LOTS OF LOFT
— ROUNDED
EDGE AND
FLAT LIE

THE SPLASH SHOT

Play the splash shot from out of a bunker around the green when the ball is sitting up reasonably well on the sand. Holding the clubface open for added loft, the idea is to splash out both ball and sand with a very full slow swing.

Set your feet with the ball well forward in the stance and the shaft of the club straight up toward you to give maximum loft. Then set the clubface open and grip it, with the leading edge of the club about 1½ inches behind the ball.

Look at the spot in the sand about 1 inch behind the ball and keep your eyes on this right through the swing. Never look directly at the ball or you will catch it too cleanly and send it too far.

Use a full slow swing, saying to yourself: "All the way back and all the way through." Feel the club splashing through the sand and out beyond the ball, keeping your wrists firm and resisting

any temptation to flick at the ball or whip the clubhead through at speed. The swing should feel like an ordinary full swing, but with no wrist action through impact.

Good players hold the clubface open through impact by keeping the left wrist in front and allowing the left elbow to lead through and beyond impact rather than folding away as it does in an ordinary full swing. This curbs the speed of the clubhead and provides them with greater control.

When playing a bunker shot remember that you must not touch the sand at address. However, you need to start with the clubhead low to the sand.

Learn to play the splash shot by teeing the ball up on a mound of sand and trying to slide the clubhead underneath it. Feel the club sitting open, as though lying on its back, and try to pass it beneath the ball as if you were aiming to miss the ball

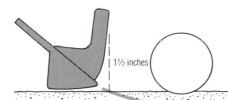

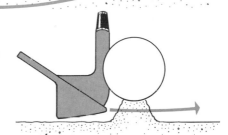

1½ inches

To splash the ball out **(above),** look 1 to 1½ inches behind the ball and splash through and out beyond it. The flange of the sand wedge bounces to help restrict the length and produce a short shot. To learn splash shots, perch the ball up on the sand **(right),** open the clubface and get the feeling that you are passing the clubhead beneath the ball.

altogether. This way you will learn to hold the clubface open and get plenty of backspin and height to the shot. Gradually get used to doing this from a flat, but still a good, lie.

The ideal length to practise this shot is 10 to 12 yards.

105

The splash shot, played with the clubface open and the ball forward in the stance. Use a full swing, holding the clubface open through impact with restricted wrist action. As you swing, your weight moves through on to the left foot.

REMEMBER
LOOK AT
THE SAND
– NEVER
THE BALL

DIRECTION IN A BUNKER

To play the splash shot you need to open the clubface for extra loft. When you do this, the face will automatically aim out to the right. Most of the problems caused with bunker shots are ones concerning the direction of the swing.

First, stand with the clubface square and your feet parallel to the line of the shot. Now open the clubface out – no more than 10 degrees – by rotating the top of the shaft and then regripping it. Turn the line of your feet and the club until the bottom of the clubface once again aims on target.

Ideally, in doing this you should turn your shoulders much less than you turn your feet so that they still remain more or less on line with the shot. Then you should feel that you are swinging the club up and down in the line of the shot and

Set the clubface open for added loft. Then turn the address position, swinging left to counteract this, and pop the ball out on target. Professionals also hold the clubface open and cut under and across it a little more at impact to add height and backspin. If anything, you will find yourself right of target with bunker shots. Monitor results and adjust the feel as necessary.

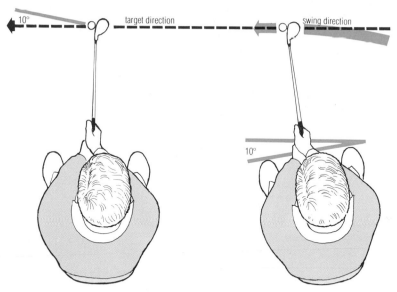

To open the clubface, turn it to the right about 10 degrees and grip the club. Then turn yourself and the club around until the bottom groove aims on target once again. Your feet will now be open **(right)**, that is left of the target. Ensure that the ball is kept far enough forward in the stance and toward the toe rather than the neck of the club.

not following the direction of your feet.

In reality, many professionals swing out-to-in in relation to the direction of the shot. Club players often swing too much out-to-in. As a result they tend to have an awkward feeling of swinging across their body.

When in a bunker, the expression "swinging out-to-in" means swinging slightly out-to-in in relation to the direction of the shot – not in relation to the direction of the feet.

When you first learn the splash shot, keep it uncomplicated. Simply open the clubface and be prepared for the ball to keep popping out to the right. Gradually, and with practice, you will learn to aim yourself around to the left to counteract this without the awkward feeling of being excessively out-to-in.

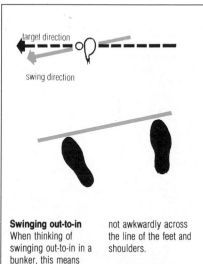

Swinging out-to-in When thinking of swinging out-to-in in a bunker, this means out-to-in in relation to the line to the target, not awkwardly across the line of the feet and shoulders.

REMEMBER
BALL TOWARD TOE OF CLUB WHEN YOU OPEN FACE

THE EXPLOSION SHOT

Professional golfers use the explosion shot when the ball is buried in the sand or lying in a footprint. To play this shot, set the ball up centrally in the stance, with your hands ahead of it and your eyes focused in the sand about $\frac{1}{2}$ inch behind it. Keep the clubface square or slightly closed. Use a fairly wide stance so that you can transfer your weight well to the left in the throughswing.

With your hands down and forward at the address, you have a ready-made wrist cock. Add to this slightly in the backswing, keeping left-hand control, and then shift your weight to the left through impact, forcing the ball up and out.

Never try to feel you are lifting the ball or you will hang back on the right foot and catch the sand too early. Move through on the left foot and force the ball out. You should feel 95 percent of your weight on the left foot at the end of the shot, with the wrists remaining firm.

As a club player, you can use this explosion shot even from a good lie around the green. It does not have the finesse of a splash shot, but is often an easier way out of trouble for the high handicap player.

The shot is more or less like a punching action. The clubhead always enters the sand behind the ball to allow the sand to cushion the blow. Once again, look at the sand about 1 inch behind the ball, rather than looking at the ball, and

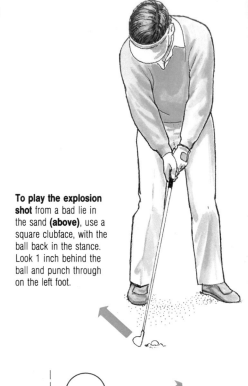

To play the explosion shot from a bad lie in the sand **(above)**, use a square clubface, with the ball back in the stance. Look 1 inch behind the ball and punch through on the left foot.

Play a ball that is buried in the sand **(above)** with a downward attack.

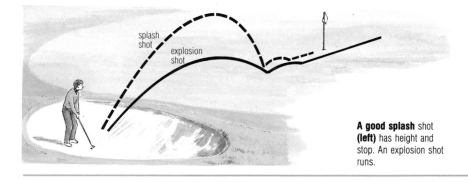

splash shot

explosion shot

A good splash shot **(left)** has height and stop. An explosion shot runs.

109

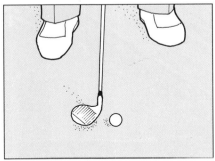

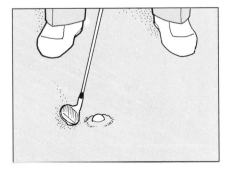

transfer your weight right through on to the left foot.

While the splash shot gives you height with plenty of stop, the explosion shot will travel lower and with more run. If the ball is buried, don't expect height and stop. Make sure that you aim for a part of the green where there is enough room for the ball to run.

The set-up for a splash shot and also for an explosion shot. With the splash shot **(left)**, the ball is forward in the stance and the clubface and stance are open. With the explosion shot **(right)** the clubface is square and the ball back in the stance.

REMEMBER
CLUBFACE
SQUARE,
WEIGHT
MOVES LEFT

DISTANCE FROM A BUNKER

A good average distance to practise a splash shot is about 12 yards. This will get you out of most greenside bunkers without running through the other side. Once you can play this standard length accurately, you can begin to vary the distance.

The short shot, of about 8 yards, is very hard to play. Good players open the clubface and swing extremely slowly and possibly slightly shorter. For the medium handicap player it is best to try taking more sand. The high handicap player should aim for the standard 12-yard shot and hope to produce a short one!

For the longer shot, of about 20 yards, an easy way out is to play the splash shot but with a square clubface, splashing through the sand as usual. This will give you more length and a little more run.

With a long bunker shot – in the 30- to 60-yard range – play as you would for a standard long pitch, with the hands slightly ahead of the ball, taking the ball and then the sand.

Up to 45 yards, it is best to use a sand wedge, moving up to a pitching wedge for the slightly longer shot. In this case, focus your eyes on the ball itself rather than the sand. This shot is like a fairway pitch.

You should approach a bunker shot of 100 yards or more as you would a fairway iron shot. If you have a perfect lie, you can hit the ball quite cleanly, looking not just at the back but slightly higher on the ball than usual. In this case, always look at the bank in front of you and do not be over-ambitious.

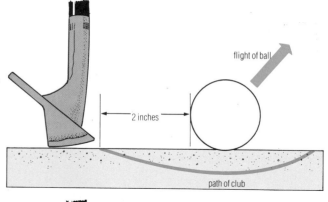

When aiming to hit 8 yards or so, professionals shorten the swing and slow it down. It is far simpler and safer to aim say 2 inches behind the ball. More sand cushions the blow.

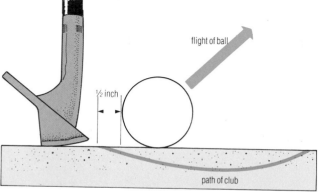

When going for about 20 yards, use a splash shot with a square rather than open clubface. Or look closer to the ball — about $\frac{1}{2}$ inch — and take less sand.

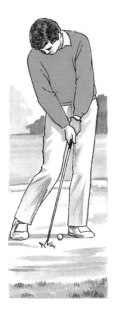

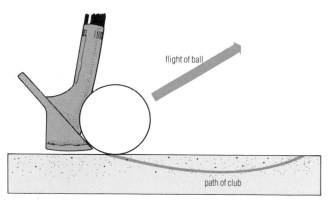

flight of ball

path of club

If you are not sure how much elevation you are going to get, take a more lofted club. With a slightly thin contact, you can hit the ball a little lower than normal – and a little farther.

If the ball sits perfectly, you can even take a wood, providing that the bank is low and you hit the ball without any sand. If the ball is sitting down in the sand, approach it as for a fairway iron shot, with your hands slightly forward, and catch the ball and then the sand beyond it.

For 30- to 60-yard shots, play with the ball back and hands forward and hit down through the ball and then the sand – like a fairway pitch.

With a long bunker shot, from a perfect lie just aim to hit the ball cleanly. From a poorer lie, hit ball and then sand. Take enough loft to negotiate the lip.

111

REMEMBER
TAKE BALL
CLEANLY FOR
MAXIMUM
LENGTH

UNDER THE BUNKER FACE

Club golfers often worry unnecessarily about a ball that is positioned in the face of a bunker. In fact, this is one of the easiest shots to play.

The slope of the bunker face is like a launch pad and sets the ball off upward. However hard you hit it, the ball will not travel too far. Lean into the bank, focus your eyes on the back of the ball, and smash into it firmly. The ball will be forced more or less straight upward.

Occasionally you may be unlucky – for instance if the slope is just too steep to negotiate easily. But the shot itself is simple to execute. Just lean into the bank and hit firmly into it.

The correct etiquette is to enter the bunker from the back – never the front. If, however, you have a very steep bunker face, sometimes the easiest way of setting

up is to enter the bunker from above. If necessary, you may have to go down on your left knee and edge your right foot down on to the sand. This stance also avoids making too many footprints in the sand, an important consideration in case the ball does not get out but rolls back in. Grip down the club and keep your weight on the left side.

The difficult shot under the lip is one in which you are forced to stand outside the bunker with the ball inside, and positioned below your feet.

You need to settle low to play this shot, standing with your feet wide apart and your knees knocked inward, *not* forward, to give yourself room to swing. Then play the shot as normal, looking at the sand and not the ball. Make sure you stay well down at impact.

When playing a ball under the bunker face, lean into the bank. Concentrate on the back of the ball and hit firmly into it to send the ball up in the air.

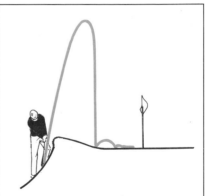

HIT IT HARD!
It does not matter how hard you hit the ball from a steep slope, since it will pop up more or less vertically and hopefully land on top of the bank and kick forward.

When the ball is under the lip of the bunker **(above)**, play the shot from outside, with your feet apart and knees together.

When the bunker face is very steep **(right)**, you may have to settle on your left knee, with your right foot in the sand. Use a lower grip and put your weight on the left side.

REMEMBER
LEAN INTO THE FACE TO FORCE THE BALL OUT

DOWNHILL SHOTS

The difficulty of any downhill shot is that the ground gets in the way of the backswing and downswing and the effect of the club loft is reduced. With a long shot the ball flies lower than normal and will curve away to the right. So take a more lofted club than usual – a 6 iron instead of a 4 iron – and aim well left of the target.

To play the shot, lean out at a right angle from the slope, so that your weight is more on the left foot, and play the ball well back in the stance. Make sure that you stay down and watch the ball through impact; it will fly off low. Don't attempt a long iron from a downhill slope. A 5 wood may be possible, but unless you are a good player, 3 or 4 woods will be difficult.

With a short downhill pitch, take a club with plenty of loft – a sand wedge. Again, the ball will set off lower and run more than normal. Lean out from the slope, so that your weight really does favour the left foot, and carry your right shoulder high at address.

Swing up and down the slope, making

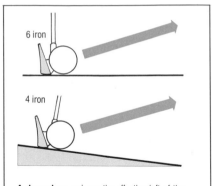

A downslope reduces the effective loft of the club. It will turn a 6 iron into a 4 iron loft and make long irons and fairway woods very difficult to use.

With a downhill shot (below), play the ball back in the stance and lean out from the slope, with your right shoulder high. Aim left and expect the ball to go low and fade away to the right.

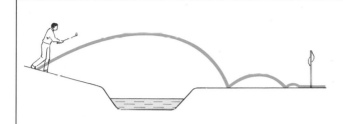

With a short shot from a downslope the ball will fly lower than normal, so use a club with plenty of loft — the sand wedge. Allow for the ball to run much more than normal on landing.

sure the club travels downward beyond impact. You will need to set your feet wide apart and have the ball back in the stance so that you definitely catch the ball without the ground getting in the way. And remember – the ball will run on landing.

For a downhill bunker shot, once again play the ball well back in the stance. Use a wide stance and make sure that the weight favours the left foot. Keep your shoulders parallel to the slope and, in

particular, keep your right shoulder high. This enables you to swing up and down the slope.

Open the clubface as much as you dare and focus your eyes about 1 inch behind the ball. The ball will not come up with much height, so aim for a low part of the bunker. Even a well-hit bunker shot from a downhill lie will run considerably, so allow for this and aim away from any other bunker or hazard on the other side of the green.

With the downhill pitch or bunker shots **(left)**, play the ball back in the stance, with the clubface open and your right shoulder high. Use a wide stance for balance and swing up and then down the slope. Try to follow through down the slope. Allow for loss of height and extra run.

short shot from downslope

bunker shot

REMEMBER SHOULDERS FOLLOWING THE SLOPE, BALL BACK

UPHILL SHOTS

When playing long uphill shots, use a wood or very long iron and lean out from the slope, swinging the club up it. You can play the ball well forward in the stance, toward the left foot. Be prepared for the ball to travel high, with a tendency to fly away to the left.

For club players, the easiest lie is often on a slight uphill slope. This type of lie tends to stop any slice and encourage good height on the shot. The opposite can be true for professionals and low handicap golfers, since it aggravates any tendency to hook the ball. If this is the case, you may need to aim to the right to allow for the ball to travel slightly left.

For those shots in which you are using anything from a 5 iron up to a wedge, the easiest approach is to lean into the slope, keeping the weight on your left foot, and

For long shots with a wood, lean out from the slope and swing down and up it. The ball tends to go high and fly left. This is an easy shot for amateurs, and stops any slice, but is often harder for professionals than a downslope shot because it aggravates the hook.

For an iron shot, lean into the slope and keep the weight on your left foot throughout. Punch the ball away, and it will go off as usual. It is vital to sway to the left through impact.

116

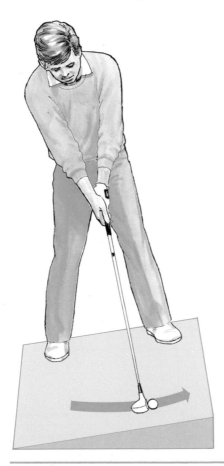

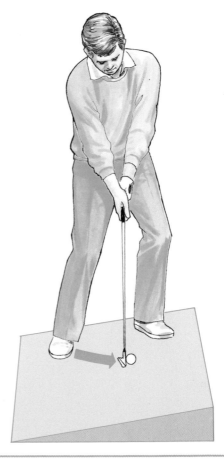

punch the ball away, taking the ball and a divot. The ball will fly off as usual, if you really do almost sway to the left through impact. Any tendency to fall back will encourage the ball to go to the left.

When hitting uphill, always take plenty of club. The ball will tend to fly high and lose distance. Remember, however, that if you are hitting to a green above you, the ball does not land vertically but touches down while still travelling forward and is likely to run too much.

So beware the elevated green. The ball will either land short and roll back or land on the green and run through. Do not under-club. Be prepared to play to the back of the green.

When you are pitching from an uphill lie just around the green, the ball will pop up high and it is very easy to leave it short, not least because the slope exaggerates the loft of the club. Talk yourself into passing the flag and, instead of taking a sand wedge in this situation, use a 9 iron or pitching wedge to achieve the same height.

COPING WITH UPHILL LIES
There are two approaches to uphill lies:
1 Using a long club, sweep the ball up the slope and expect it to go to the left.
2 With shorter shots, lean into the slope, punch into it and expect a normal flight.

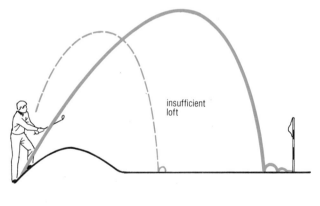

insufficient loft

When pitching from an upslope around the green, the ball will pop up high; it is easy to misjudge this and leave the ball short. The slope exaggerates the loft of the club. Give it enough and always aim at passing the hole. Take a less lofted club if necessary — a 9 iron instead of a wedge — to keep the ball moving forward.

(117)

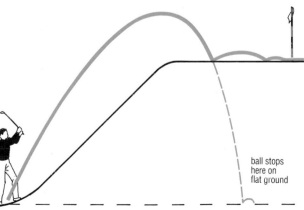

ball stops here on flat ground

When hitting uphill, take plenty of club. Remember the ball goes high off an upslope. BUT, instead of landing nearly vertically, it touches down and runs forward. Always expect a ball to run to the back of an elevated green and don't under-club.

REMEMBER
THE BALL
WILL RUN ON
AN ELEVATED
GREEN

SIDEHILL LIES

Ideally you should practise playing sidehill shots from flat lies to encourage a good golf swing. Be aware, however, of what happens from sidehill lies.

When you take up your stance with the ball below your feet, this is going to bring out the worst in your swing if you tend to slice or, even worse, shank. It forces you to bend over more and tends to produce a high, upright swing which will send that ball slicing away to the right.

Allow the swing to be more upright, but check that you keep the ball toward the toe of the club. Maintain balance through impact, stay down and watch the ball very carefully.

The ball will slice away to the right. Remember, too, that it will spin farther right when it lands. To aggravate this, the chances are that it will be landing on

Stand above the ball (left) and it will tend to move left-to-right in flight and then kick right on landing.

Stand below the ball (right) and it tends to move right-to-left in flight and kick left on landing.

ground that is also sloping away to the right, in which case it will kick off even farther.

Most players do not aim far enough left when playing this shot. Allow for the ball to curve, spin and then kick — and always aim it well left of the green.

When you are standing below the ball, you will be aggravating any tendency to hook or pull it. Grip an inch or two down the club for extra control and remember that your swing will now be flat and around your body. You will tend to pull

the ball away to your left, which can pose problems for the player who hooks.

Again, you will have to aim more to the right, allowing for the curve in flight, for the spin on landing, and for the lie of the land throwing the ball even farther left.

The easiest way to remember which direction the ball will move in is to bear in mind that it bends in the air in the same way as it would roll on the ground. From above it will roll – and curve – to the right; from below it will roll – and curve – to the left.

119

REMEMBER
FOR SIDEHILL
LIES AIM
WELL UP

BANKS AND HOW TO NEGOTIATE THEM

When faced with a bank around the green, the simplest way of negotiating it is to use a putter, particularly where the ground around the ball is bare or even slightly rough, and if the flag is close to the edge of the green just over the bank.

If the grass is too fluffy to putt the ball, then consider playing a running shot with a 5 or 6 iron. You need to get the ball down on the ground quickly, before the bank, so it runs smoothly up or down it.

If the bank is steep but smooth, and the flag is just over the top of it, you can use a 4 iron, for example, to punch the ball at

the bank. The ball should pop up and over the bank. This is a risky shot but can be very useful particularly if there are overhanging trees that would make a wedge shot impossible.

Try to avoid playing the wedge unless you have a good lie to pitch from. In this situation, always try to pitch the ball on the flat part of the green, to avoid catching any downslope.

If you are playing up or down a two-tier green, always try to run the ball to the second tier rather than pitching it. This is particularly useful when the flag

Use a putter whenever possible. It is the simplest method. If the grass is at all fluffy, or you are faced with a longer shot, run the ball with a 5 or 6 iron.

If the bank is steep, but smooth, and the flag is just over it, you can try punching the ball at the bank with a 4 iron. It should pop up and over.

When playing up a smooth bank or on to a two-tier green, a running shot is generally best, particularly if the flag is near the bank. Professionals only use a wedge if they have plenty of landing space. Club golfers are generally still safer playing a running shot.

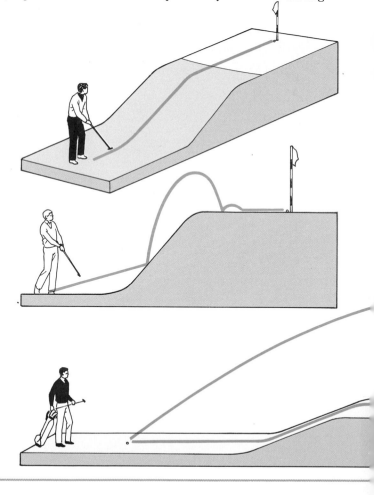

is just on the top of the second tier. Pitching on the top would be decidedly difficult; running it can, by contrast, be fairly straightforward.

When you are hitting on to an elevated green, the ball will land fairly flat and tend to run through. Also remember that this type of green often drains well and will not hold. So be prepared to finish at the back of the green. When you finish there one day, the tendency next time is to under-club and fall short.

If you are playing on to a basin green, the ball will land vertically and should stop well. The green may also hold water and therefore be slow. One danger of hitting to a basin green is pitching the ball short and catching the downslope. In this case the ball tends to run through and the temptation is to under club even more the next time. Be bold and try to hit to the flat part of the green.

When putting on a two-tier green, you may find it hard to judge the line across the slope. Mentally draw a line at right angles to the slope. This may help you read the slope and see which way you are travelling across it.

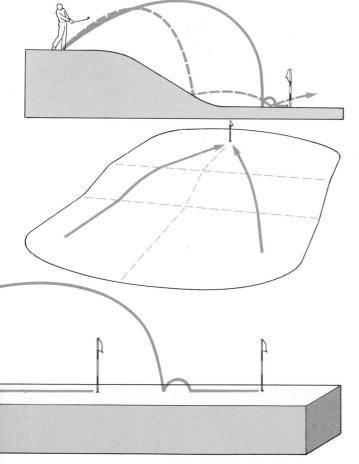

When hitting into a basin green, expect the ball to stop well. Be bold and avoid landing on the downslope.

121

On a steep, two-tier green, mentally draw a line at right angles to the slope. If putting from left of this, the putt is left-to-right; if from the right, then the putt is right-to-left. Follow clearly which way it will turn on the bank itself.

REMEMBER
WITH A BANK
THINK OF
RUNNING
THE SHOT

PUNCH SHOTS

Professional golfers do not always play full shots. Often they will use a shorter swing and punch the ball to keep it driving forward, for example when it is windy. To do this they use a shorter club. This means that instead of an 8 iron, they would punch with a 7 – or a 4 iron instead of a 5, and so on. You can use the punch shot with any club from a 3 iron to a pitching wedge.

The technique is similar to that for the long pitch, playing the ball back in the stance, hands forward and the clubface square. The backswing is solid with a short punchy finish and the wrists firm.

Particular uses for the punch shot include playing into the wind, hitting a ball that is positioned beneath tree branches or getting the ball running. It can also be a good shot for playing up a two-tier green or on to the back of a green.

With the ball back in the stance you may have to turn your feet to the left, as with long pitching, and aim left to keep the ball flying straight. As with pitching, it is not simply a question of aiming the line across the toes to the left, but often of turning both feet, paying particular attention to the right foot, to encourage

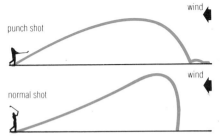

The punch shot is aimed at keeping the ball "driving" forward and is useful for penetrating a headwind **(left)**.

With a headwind, a wedge shot is all too easily blown back and off line. A punch shot with an 8 or 9 iron will keep the ball travelling forward. When playing to a green with bunkers on either side **(left)**, use a punch shot and run the ball safely through the gap, perhaps using a 6 iron, rather than getting the ball up high. Remember, a headwind increases the height of the shot.

To play the punch shot (right), using anything from a 3 iron to a pitching wedge, keep the ball back in the stance, with the clubface square and your hands forward. Take a firm backswing and short punchy finish.

122

the correct direction of swing. You can
turn your feet to the left, but if you do
this you must be sure to keep your
shoulders square.

Punch shots are well worth practising,
particularly for use in adverse weather
conditions and for recovery shots. Very
often you can gain the same sort of length
with a punch shot as you would from a
full swing with the same club.

With experience you can then learn to
play these shots holding the clubface
slightly closed or open through impact to
bend the ball slightly to the left or to the
right, respectively.

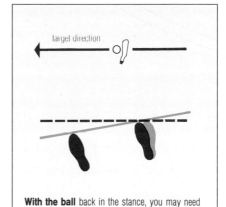

With the ball back in the stance, you may need
to turn your feet to the left and aim them left to
keep the ball flying straight. Note that the right
foot is turned in and not straight in front.

(123)

PLAYING FROM THE ROUGH

The wedges are the heaviest clubs in the set. With a bad lie in the rough, you can use a wedge to cut through the grass. From a very heavy rough, take the shortest route to the fairway and always with the wedge.

When playing this type of shot, have the ball back in the stance, with your hands forward and your weight more on to the left foot. Adopt a fairly wide stance so you can transfer your weight easily.

The club needs to accelerate smoothly through the ball. The danger is to take too long a swing and decelerate. Grip the club very tightly and concentrate on a smooth slow swing, back and through. Your backswing and throughswing should be roughly the same length.

Make sure you keep the club moving through impact. As with all short shots, keep your head perfectly still and try to listen for the ball to land rather than looking up to watch it come down.

Think sensibly about position for your

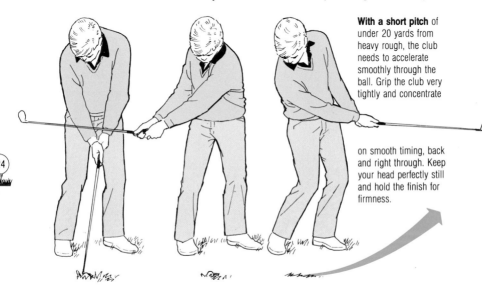

With a short pitch of under 20 yards from heavy rough, the club needs to accelerate smoothly through the ball. Grip the club very tightly and concentrate

on smooth timing, back and right through. Keep your head perfectly still and hold the finish for firmness.

THE GOLDEN RULE
When playing a recovery shot, always take the shortest route back to the fairway. In this case the player cannot reach the green and so must get in the best position for the next shot. Use the weight of the wedge to get out safely.

next shot and do not be over-ambitious. If you cannot get on the green with your recovery shot, make sure that you play into a safe position.

From medium rough, play with the ball back in the stance, hitting down and through it, once again with your weight more on to the left foot for a downward attack. Make sure that your head stays still and your wrists remain firm. Once again, think about where the ball is going to finish, looking for a flat area and one

that is not going to be impeded by trees.

From light heather or rough, you can use a 4 or 5 wood to gain extra length. Keep a firm grip so that the club does not twist through impact. Do not be greedy. If you cannot reach the green with your best shot, do not attempt the wood shot if you have nothing else to gain.

When recovering from the rough, play the ball farther back in the stance for a downward attack, with your weight favouring the left foot. Hit down and watch the ball intently.

125

BAD LIES

When you find yourself with a bad lie, the secret of recovery is often in the right choice of club, with the relevant action. Here are a few typical examples of how to cope in different situations.

An iron shot from a divot hole
As with all recovery shots, you must move your weight more on to the left foot, hitting the ball with a downward attack. The ball may travel slightly lower than normal and is likely to finish right of the target. So be sure to aim left and take a more lofted club.

Because you cannot get under a golf ball, do not try to help it up. The worse the lie, the farther back in the stance you should play the ball. If necessary, set your feet left of the target.

A wood shot from a poor lie
Sometimes a small-headed fairway wood fits more easily into a divot hole than a long iron. You can help this by tipping the head of the club slightly forward to get the back of the sole off the ground. Play the ball farther back in the stance than normal for a slightly downward attack. Squeeze the ball out with a tiny divot.

Playing from a tight bare lie
This type of lie, in which you have no cushion of grass beneath the ball, can be difficult. The tighter the lie, the better your judgement of depth needs to be. With an iron shot from a bare lie, your weight should be more on to the left foot. You must remember to hit down and through the ball.

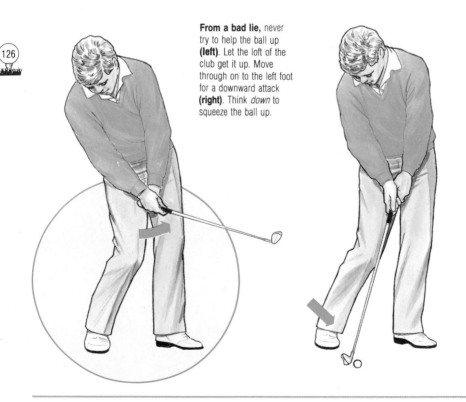

From a bad lie, never try to help the ball up **(left)**. Let the loft of the club get it up. Move through on to the left foot for a downward attack **(right)**. Think *down* to squeeze the ball up.

Take a similar approach with a long pitch from a bare lie. With a short pitch of 15 yards or so, a bare lie can be difficult. Take two or three practice swings to get the depth right and *listen* for the clubhead bouncing on the ground. Always concentrate on depth in the swing.

With a fairway wood from a tight lie, the main point is again good judgement of depth. As with a short pitch, take two or three practice swings and make sure that the sole of the club bounces on the ground. If the practice swing is not right, then take time to repeat it. Remember that from a bare lie depth is crucial.

A long pitch from a divot hole

As with a basic iron shot, this should be fairly straightforward, provided you hit down and take the ball first and then the divot. With a longish pitch, it is fairly easy to accelerate through the ball and transfer your weight to the left foot. When you are playing a medium length shot, it is quite simple to decelerate instead of accelerate. As the shot becomes shorter, restrict the length of the backswing but still accelerate smoothly through the ball and divot.

A short pitch from a divot hole

The very short pitch, from 10 to 20 yards, out of a divot is difficult, even for professional golfers. One way of tackling it is to consider balancing the sand wedge on its toe. The rounded toe may get into the hole where the sole of the club will not. If you watch the ball very carefully, you may be able to tweak it out with some success.

More advanced players sometimes play this type of shot by adopting a V-shaped attack. With their weight on the left foot, they lift the club up sharply but slowly with the wrists, then swing it down and up again, hingeing up from the left elbow. Remember that the shorter the shot from a bad lie, the more difficult it usually becomes.

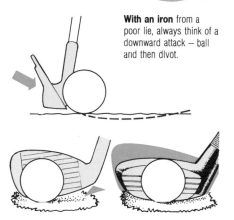

With an iron from a poor lie, always think of a downward attack — ball and then divot.

With a short pitch from a divot hole, think of balancing the clubhead toward its toe **(above left)**. This may help you find the bottom of the ball. A small-headed fairway wood **(above right)** can be easier than a long iron when playing from a divot.

127

Advanced players use a sand wedge for a 10- to 15-yard pitch from a bad lie. They lift the club with wrist action in the backswing, holding on to this wrist cock and then make a V-shaped attack with their wrists firm, but picking up the club by hingeing from their left elbow.

REMEMBER
THINK DOWN
TO GET THE
BALL UP

EXPERT DRIVING

Here are some important tips to help you improve your driving off the tee.

● Plan the line and length of your target carefully. Ideally choose a target not only on the line you want but roughly the length you want. This will usually prove more successful than choosing an object on the horizon. If there is no target there, imagine a bullseye on the fairway where you want the ball to land.

To judge the line, do not merely look at the obstacles to either side and try to go between them. On a tight drive, always choose a specific point. It focuses your mind on a positive approach.

● Always aim away from any major trouble area. If there is a bunker at driving distance, don't just aim 5 yards away from it. Be prepared to aim about 20 yards away and allow yourself a greater margin for error.

● Concentrate on balance and finish. Every player is nervous on the first tee. Often people will only watch you here and

will only see that shot. Always concentrate on making the swing look good, watch the ball carefully and work for a balanced finish.

● When playing a long hole, or when an opponent drives farther than you do, never try to hit the ball too hard. Concentrate on good timing and hit the ball your normal distance. If you press for length, your direction tends to go. Swing smoothly in order to achieve maximum length and control.

● If playing for safety, take a shorter club, such as a 3 iron or 4 wood, and hit firmly. Never take a driver and try to steer the ball with a half-hearted swing. Playing safe does not mean that you have to be negative.

● As your standard improves, learn to play safe drives by bending the ball slightly, particularly from left to right. Skilful golfers will fade the ball away from trouble on the left by holding the clubface slightly open through impact and slowing down any hand and wrist action. They aim the stance and swing where they want to start the ball and allow it to drift slightly right. This approach is particularly important for those who tend to hook the ball.

Never look at or think about what you are trying to avoid. Always imagine a target to aim at in order to achieve optimum line and length.

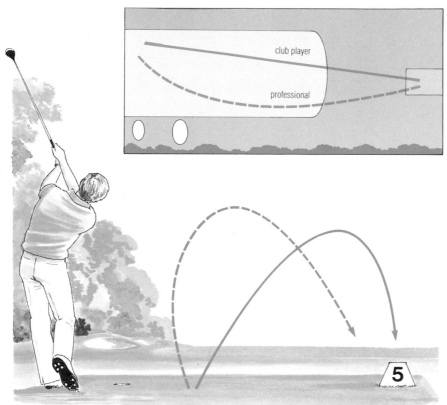

129

5

With trouble down the left, the professional usually tries to aim toward it and fade the ball away from it. In contrast the club golfer should turn to aim away from it **(above)**.

Vary the height at which you tee the ball up **(below)**. More height helps keep the ball left; less height helps keep it right. Always select the flattest lie on the tee.

● Do not forget that you can tread down the ground behind the ball and pick pieces of grass on the tee, where you cannot do this elsewhere. Tee the ball up at a consistent height, but remember that to help keep the drive to the right you can tee it lower than normal. Conversely, to help a ball keep left you can tee it slightly higher than normal.

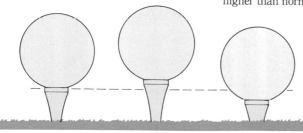

REMEMBER BALANCE AND TIMING FOR EXPERT DRIVING

GAMBLING AND STRATEGY

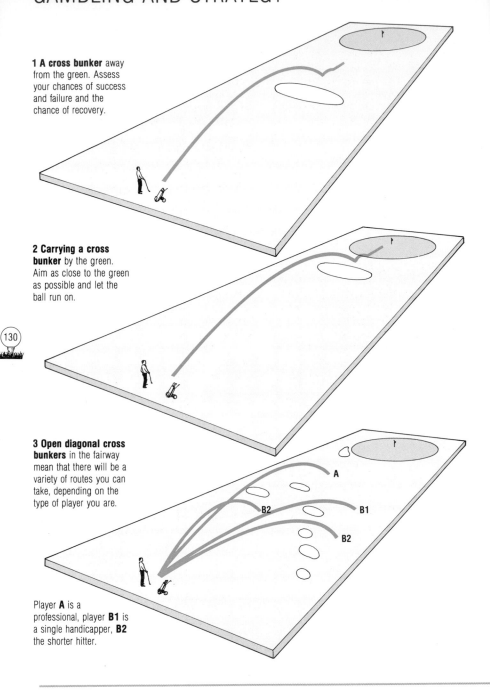

1 A cross bunker away from the green. Assess your chances of success and failure and the chance of recovery.

2 Carrying a cross bunker by the green. Aim as close to the green as possible and let the ball run on.

3 Open diagonal cross bunkers in the fairway mean that there will be a variety of routes you can take, depending on the type of player you are.

Player **A** is a professional, player **B1** is a single handicapper, **B2** the shorter hitter.

Sound thinking on the course means weighing up what you stand to achieve by taking a risk. Don't go for a carry over trees, for example, just because they are a challenge and if you are unlikely to gain any advantage. And do not play a risky recovery shot if success only gains 10 or 20 yards over the safe shot.

Cross bunkers

With bunkers across the fairway, know precisely where you need to be to carry them. If you are unsure, look at what you might gain with success or how you could suffer from failure. Here are three situations to give you an idea of the alternatives in different bunker settings.

In Situation **1** (illustration, left), you may be able to carry the bunker, but cannot reach the green. The question you need to ask is whether you could get out of the bunker on to the green. In this case, the bunker is too deep and far away. So the gamble is not worth taking.

In Situation **2**, success would put you on the green. You have determined that the bunker is shallow and that you could

recover on to the green if you failed to make the carry.

In a similar situation, but with a deep bunker, you cannot recover on to the green. Whether you attempt the carry will depend on precise knowledge of distance, any headwind, possibly the pin position and the state of the match.

Diagonal trouble

With diagonal bunkers, Situation **3**, or where there is a stream across the fairway, be prepared to zig-zag to the green. Good golfers regularly hit away from the flag more often than club golfers.

The professional (player A) can carry the bunkers and will look for position. This will depend on where the pin is sited and how close it is to the left-hand bunker. The single handicapper (player B1) can make the carry on the right-hand side, but not the left. This also gives a clear view of the flag. The shorter hitter (player B2) cannot carry the end bunkers and should look for position up the middle or out to the right, over what he can carry and where there is a good line to the flag.

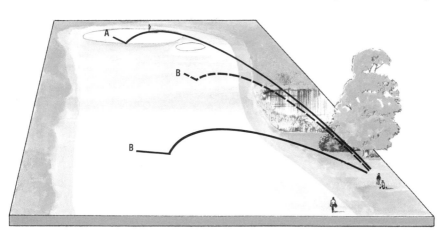

Player A stands to gain something with this recovery shot. Success will get him on the green.

Failure will probably still leave him there with the next shot. For player **B**, the gamble (dotted line)

may not get him on to the green. A safe recovery shot will still get him there in two shots.

REMEMBER
DON'T TAKE
RISKS IF
NOTHING CAN
BE GAINED

MORE ABOUT STRATEGY

A golf course is normally full of problems and hazards. Knowing how to cope with them all is crucial for consistently good scoring. Here are just a few situations you may encounter in the course of a round and some ways in which you can cope with them successfully.

You need to think very carefully about the best way to play out of a fairway bunker, for example. Look at the distance. If you are, say, 150 yards from the hole, you will probably need a 5 iron.

Ask yourself whether you are confident you can get over the bank in front of you. If so, then have a go. If you are not sure, then don't just take a 6 iron and still risk hitting the bank. Play a little safer with a 7 or 8 iron, even if that means taking two shots to get up there. When faced with water or bunkers in front of the green,

you must again assess the risks.

You may well be able to make the carry from, say, 200 yards. But the question is whether the ball will stop if you do get over the hazard safely. Are you simply going to run into trouble over the back of the green? If so, you may finish closer by playing short and pitching up with the next shot.

When playing around the green, consider all the options; even go sideways, if necessary. A running shot to the side of the bunker may finish closer than a good pitch played over it.

Remember that if the greenkeeper has put a flag behind the bunker, he is trying to tempt you into it. Allow for a little error and go for the heart of the green or just to the side of the bunker, rather than being drawn into it.

If you are confident you can make the carry with a 5 iron from the fairway bunker to the green **(above right)**, then go for it. But to make sure, use a 7 or 8 iron and play short **(below right)**. It's probably an extra shot but reduces the risk factor.

With a 200-yard shot to the green over water or a bunker **(right)**, you may make the carry but can you stop the ball? From 150 yards, you should be able to control it, and the long shot is worth playing. Consider this if the green has a severe slope. If you play the long shot to the green, the ball may kick off to the side. By playing up short to the front of the green, you give yourself a safer, straightforward chip.

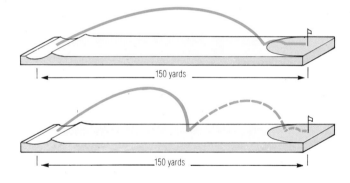

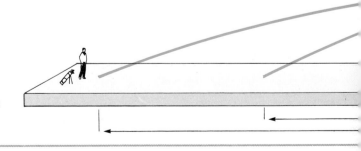

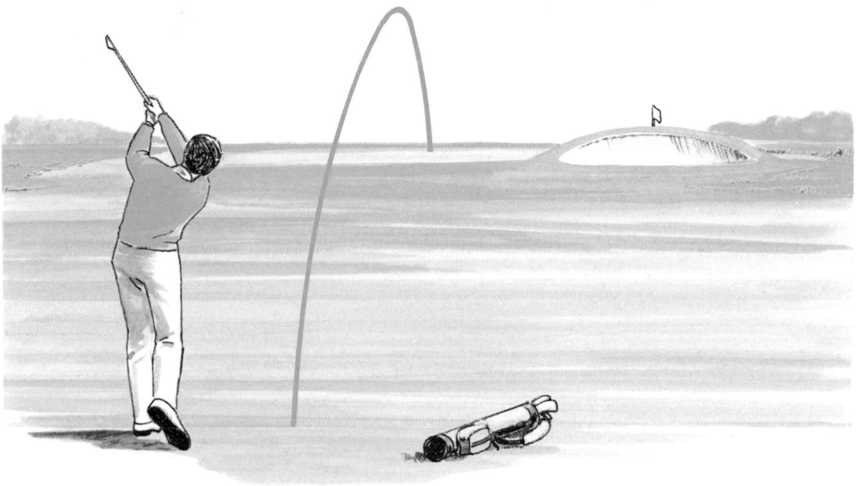

Avoid the greenkeeper's trap when the flag is tucked behind a bunker **(above)**. Go for the heart of the green or just to the side.

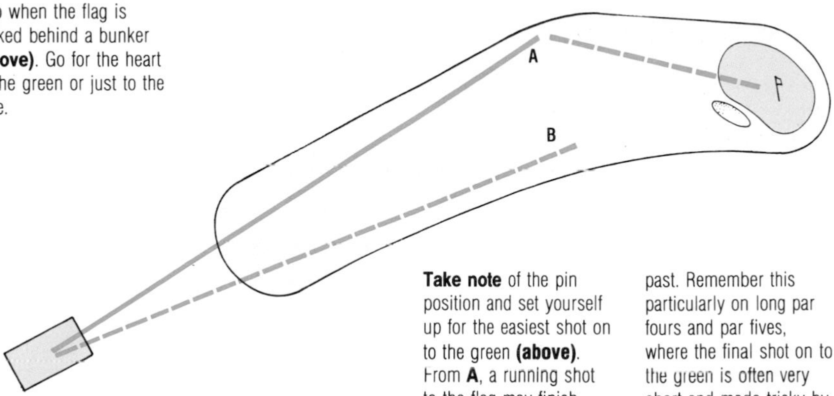

(133)

Take note of the pin position and set yourself up for the easiest shot on to the green **(above)**. From **A**, a running shot to the flag may finish closer than a pitch shot from **B**, which could run past. Remember this particularly on long par fours and par fives, where the final shot on to the green is often very short and made tricky by the position of the flag in relation to the bunker.

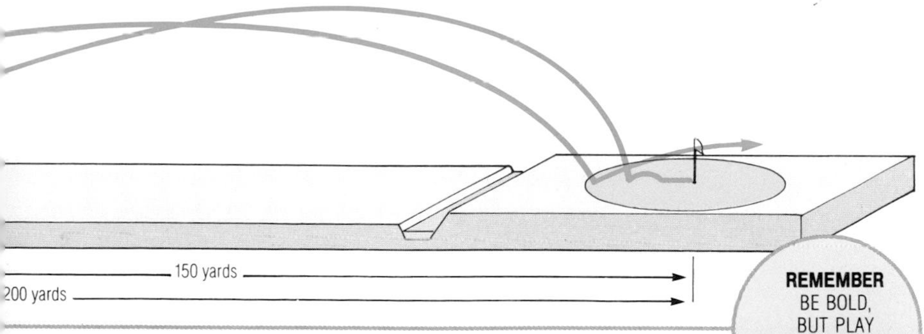

150 yards

200 yards

REMEMBER
BE BOLD,
BUT PLAY
SAFE WHEN
NECESSARY

PAR THREES

An important point to remember about par threes is that you can change the view you get of the flag – often quite dramatically – by choosing the spot from which to tee the ball. What you see from the left- and right-hand sides of the tee can be quite different.

Do not forget that if you feel there is a better position on the tee, you can always go back two club-lengths if you wish. This may also give you a better lie, or might even just feel easier.

When driving with an iron on a par three, push the tee well into the ground so

that the ball is as it would be on a normal, good lie. You certainly do not want it right up as it would be if you were using a driver.

Be realistic about distance, and remember that most trouble at these holes is at the front of the green. The distance shown on the tee marker should be to the centre of the green, so allow a little extra to the flag. And always take sufficient

You can change the view by choosing where to tee the ball **(below)**. You can go back two club-lengths. Do not automatically tee up in your partner's peg hole!

Tee the ball to the equivalent of a good lie **(right)** – not up in the air as for a driver.

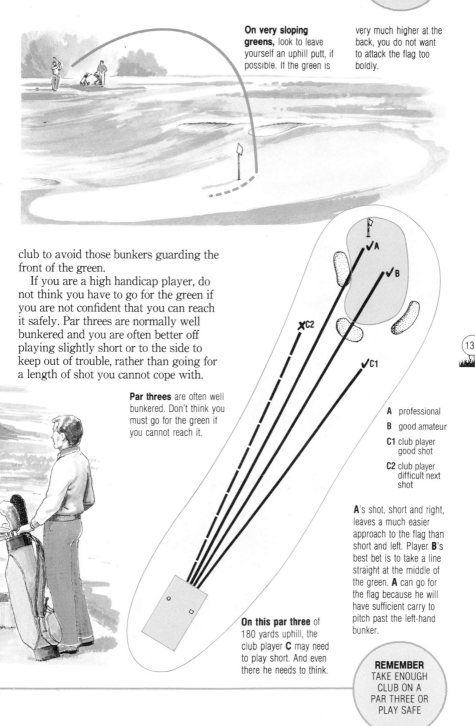

On very sloping greens, look to leave yourself an uphill putt, if possible. If the green is very much higher at the back, you do not want to attack the flag too boldly.

club to avoid those bunkers guarding the front of the green.

If you are a high handicap player, do not think you have to go for the green if you are not confident that you can reach it safely. Par threes are normally well bunkered and you are often better off playing slightly short or to the side to keep out of trouble, rather than going for a length of shot you cannot cope with.

Par threes are often well bunkered. Don't think you must go for the green if you cannot reach it.

135

A professional
B good amateur
C1 club player
   good shot
C2 club player
   difficult next
   shot

A's shot, short and right, leaves a much easier approach to the flag than short and left. Player **B**'s best bet is to take a line straight at the middle of the green. **A** can go for the flag because he will have sufficient carry to pitch past the left-hand bunker.

On this par three of 180 yards uphill, the club player **C** may need to play short. And even there he needs to think.

REMEMBER
TAKE ENOUGH
CLUB ON A
PAR THREE OR
PLAY SAFE

THE ART OF RECOVERY

If average club golfers had a professional on hand to advise them on recovery shots, they would improve dramatically. When you are out on the course, you will have to rely on your friend "Good Sense", who sits on your shoulder.

Whatever your position, ask yourself what is the sensible shot – regardless of the score. For example, if you land up in the trees, the correct, common-sense shot may be to punch the ball out on to a good lie on the fairway.

If you are doing particularly badly, do not gamble and do something stupid. Even if you are doing well, do not be over-ambitious – or, for that matter, over-cautious.

The golden rule for recovery shots is to take the shortest route back to safety. Do not try to punch the ball through the trees if you are not going to gain anything. And do not loft it over the trees only to end up in the rough.

A sound golfing saying is that any tree is 90 percent wood when it's your shot and 90 percent air when it is your opponent's!

If you recover sensibly and safely, you often find you will be rewarded by holing a good putt. If you take silly risks and get into more trouble, you are often punished by poor putting, too.

When you find yourself with a bad lie, walk out of the trouble spot and have a good look at the shot. Select a sensible target to aim for and do not rush. Plan carefully where you want to recover to, choosing if you can a simple flat area from where to play the next shot.

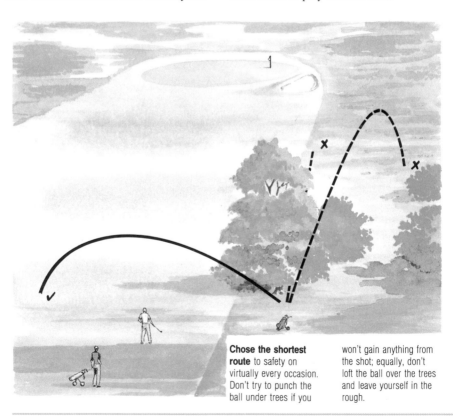

Chose the shortest route to safety on virtually every occasion. Don't try to punch the ball under trees if you won't gain anything from the shot; equally, don't loft the ball over the trees and leave yourself in the rough.

With this type of situation (above), walk out to the fairway and analyse where you want to be with your recovery shot. Position **1** is giving the player a good flat, grassy lie with an easy shot to the green. Position **2** nearer the green is not as good. Although the shot is shorter, the player is now faced with a bare, downhill lie and a much more testing shot to the green. Position **3** seems, at first glance, to offer a safe recovery shot, but the player is now faced with having to pitch the ball over a bunker to the flag.

2 club lengths

If you find yourself in bushes to the side of the fairway **(above)** and you cannot play out on to the green, do think about taking a drop under the "unplayable ball" rule. Why not pick out two club lengths away for one shot and save risking a disaster? From **B**, two club lengths gives you a clear swing and is definitely the option to take. From **A**, picking the ball out two club lengths may leave you with an impeded backswing.

When you have a bad lie, watch the ball well at impact and ask your partner or caddy to watch the shot too. Plan exactly where you want to recover to, choosing an easy, flat spot if possible. Select a proper target and be as fussy about where you aim to land your recovery shot as with any other shot.

137

REMEMBER
TAKE THE
SHORTEST
ROUTE BACK
TO SAFETY

WIND AND WEATHER

When the wind is blowing and you are getting soaked by the rain, remember that everyone else is suffering the same problem. Don't be downhearted. Just think of it as another golfing challenge.

Suitable kit is vital in the wet. Make sure you carry an umbrella, preferably a bright one to cheer you up. Keep a towel hanging inside it. If you wear glasses, fit a visor to them. Wear waterproofs that are comfortable and do not impede your swing. Always have at least one spare glove in your golf bag, preferably in a polythene bag. And finally, the best thing for keeping your hands dry are mittens.

In windy conditions, put on a hat or visor to keep your hair out of the way and wear clothing that does not flap about and distract you.

Here are some useful hints for playing in the rain:
● Keep a dry ball for driving. A wet ball dives rather than flies.
● If it is extremely wet, take your practice swings before teeing up the ball to keep it as dry as possible.
● Keep the handles of your clubs dry – and in the bag as long as possible, with a hood over that.
● While waiting for your partners to drive off, keep your club dry and return it to the bag as soon as possible after use.
● The rain can make recovery shots from the rough difficult and play havoc on the greens, which can get very slippery. As a result balls are liable to skid. As they get wetter, they lose this slipperiness and become slower.

138

The correct elevantion will come only when the ball is dry. A wet one will duck and you will lose height and carry in the shot.

dry ball

wet ball

Be prepared for the rain – and carry waterproofs in your golf bag. Jack Nicklaus makes sure he is well protected during the 1986 British Open at Turnberry.

Even a dull, wet day at Wentworth does not dampen the enthusiasm of these spectators.

139

PLAYING IN THE WIND

In windy conditions, always toss some grass up in the air to check which way the wind is blowing. Don't wait until you have played the shot and made a mistake.

Look at the flag to judge the direction of the wind and, in particular, be wary of a sheltered tee and exposed fairway or green – and vice versa. You may stand on a tee and not feel the wind. But once the ball leaves the trees, it gets blown off line.

Swing smoothly and keep perfect balance. Exaggerate this by holding your balance for at least four or five seconds. In windy conditions, the danger is for your swing to be blown off its true line.

Side wind

With a side wind, aim for a spot to the side of the target from which the wind is blowing and hit for that. Aim your stance, clubface and swing to this spot and let the wind do the rest.

If you are a low handicap player, you can try to bend the ball into the wind to hold it straight. Open or close the clubface at address, depending on the direction the wind is blowing.

Head wind

Think of a head wind adding up to four clubs to the shot and take plenty of club. Swing slowly and don't fight the wind. You are unlikely to hit through the back of the green, so go for the full distance.

When driving, offset the effect of the wind with a lower trajectory. Tee the ball a little lower and aim to leave the tee in the ground. Experienced players may aim for a slightly flatter swing plane and use a stiffer-wristed action to reduce the backswing. Good balance is vital.

140

The key thought when playing in bad weather must be to hold your balance. Exaggerate this. Swing smoothly with extra good balance and keep your swing the same throughout the 18 holes.

Beware of the shot from a sheltered tee where the fairway and green are exposed. Look at the flag to see which way the wind is blowing – and how strongly.

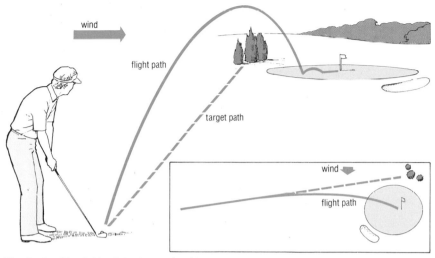

wind

flight path

target path

wind

flight path

Allow for the side wind by aiming to a new target to the side of the green. Address the clubface, stance and swing at this target and let the wind do the rest.

Remember, too, that an off-line shot tends to be exaggerated, with the ball rising and spinning more quickly.

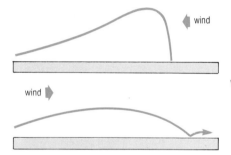

wind

wind

Down wind
Here it is important to drive the ball high enough. Tee it up to get good height and, if necessary, use a 3 wood to achieve enough elevation. This may send the ball farther than a driver. A wind from behind tends to flatten the shot and keep the ball down; it also tends to straighten out bending shots.

When playing on to the green, take off up to four clubs and remember that the ball bounces on landing. So a softer ball may stop better.

If you do go through the green, remember your pitch shot back is into the wind. Over-club through the green and the chances are you will then under-hit when coming back.

Very windy conditions can affect the ball on the green just as much as they do the long game. This is particularly so on a fast green when playing downwind.

When playing into a head wind, the ball can fly higher and be taken off line more easily. With a down wind the ball tends to go lower and, if anything, the wind will straighten out the shot.

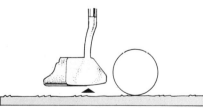

Windy conditions will also affect the way the ball rolls on the green. If it is very windy, don't ground the club in case the ball moves.

(141)

REMEMBER
EXTRA GOOD
BALANCE
IN WINDY
CONDITIONS

JUDGING DISTANCE

Judging distance and taking the correct club are essential for good scoring. So check the distances you hit the ball with each club, on par threes and on the practice ground.

If you know the distance you can hit the ball with a 5 iron – the carry through the air – assume the 6 iron will be 10 yards less, the 7 iron 20 yards less than that and so on. Be realistic and do not under-club. As a rule, average players consistently take too little club and in most conditions are short of the flag. The

shot may look good, but as you approach the green the error in distance becomes all too obvious. Under-club by one club and you then risk three putting.

Remember, too, that most trouble is to be found at the front of the green. So be bold. On courses in America, Spain and Japan, in particular, look for little trees that are often planted 150 yards or so from the centre of each green.

The more accurate your knowledge of distance, the more confidently you can strike the ball and attack the course.

Use cards and distance charts when available. These usually show the distances from specific points to the centre of each green **(right)**, as well as information about the length of the green and the position of trees

and bunkers. Trust the information, mentally adding 10 or 20 yards for up or downslopes and for a head or tailwind.

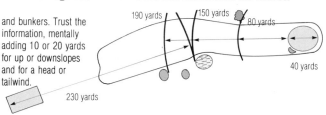

190 yards   150 yards   80 yards

40 yards

230 yards

DON'T BE DECEIVED

Certain situations can be deceptive when it comes to judging distance. Here are a few examples:

1 A flag toward the back of a green probably looks closer to the back than it really is and may tempt you to be too cautious. Look at other greens on your way round to check the flag position. Remember the deceptive greens at home.

2 Flags are not uniform in height. A tall flag can look closer than it is; a short one can make the shot look longer. Judge the green with people on it.

3 Beware of undulations that appear to be just in

front of the green. There may be 30 or 40 yards of hidden ground there. The tendency is to under-club.

4 Large bunkers can look deceptively close.

5 Very flat ground can be difficult to judge, with hidden ground and distances you just do not see.

6 Tall trees can look closer than they are or may make a flag look very small and farther away.

7 Try to judge distance with people on the green or walking to it. On a flat course, or where there is hidden ground, you can often learn about distance by counting the number of paces others take between bunkers and the green.

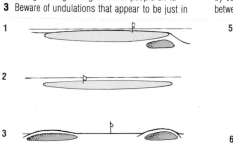

1

2

3

4

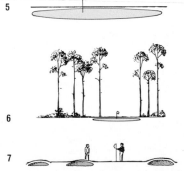

5

6

7

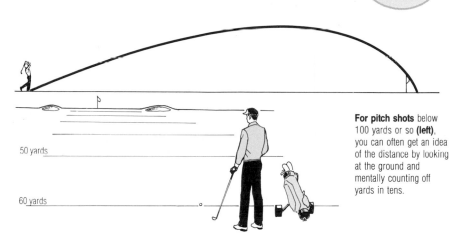

50 yards

60 yards

For pitch shots below 100 yards or so **(left)**, you can often get an idea of the distance by looking at the ground and mentally counting off yards in tens.

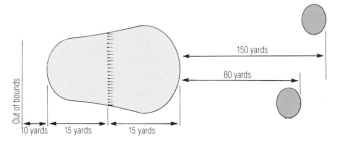

150 yards

80 yards

Out of bounds

10 yards   15 yards   15 yards

Professionals measure distances carefully in practice rounds by pacing out the yardage from key spots. Usually this includes distances from a point near the driving zone **(left)**, plus details of the depth of each green, trouble beyond the green and any deceptive slopes. Do the same on your own course.

143

On a hole with ditches or bunkers across the fairway, know the precise point from which you can make the carry under still air conditions. Make an allowance for any head or tailwind. Knowledge such as this can save strokes.

REMEMBER
ALWAYS AIM
TO PASS
THE FLAG

AIMING

The golf swing and your subsequent shots are only as good as your aiming. If your aim is poor, your shots will naturally go off line. In turn, you will find there is a tendency to counteract poor alignment by swinging badly.

Many golfers fail to aim accurately, the most common error being that of aiming off to the right of the target. This results not just in shots pushed out to the right,

but also in shots pulled round to the left.

With all golf shots, except the very short putts, you cannot see the ball and target at the same time.

The correct way of aiming in a square stance is for the line across your feet, knees, hips, shoulders and eyes to be parallel to the proposed line of the shot.

On putts of up to about 4 feet, you can see the ball and the hole with both eyes. From 4 feet up to around 8 feet, you can as a rule see both with your left eye (for right-handers) but not the right. A certain degree of distortion can, however, be expected to take place.

Above this distance you have to

4 feet   8 feet

Only with a very short putt (above) can you see the ball and the hole with both eyes — and from 4 to 8 feet with one eye only.

With all shots other than shortish putts **(right)**, you have to visualize the target and aim to a picture of that in your head. Look at the target, see it in the right place and hit to that image. Most golfers look up early — not just to see where the ball has gone but also to see where it is going — almost before impact.

target direction

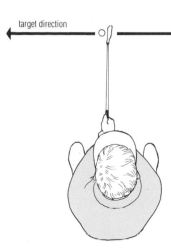

For standard shots,
stand parallel to the ball-
to-target line **(left)**. In
practice, check your
aiming with a club laid
along your toes.

**If you are having
problems** with aiming
(below), particularly if
you are going diagonally
across the fairway or

playing from a badly
aligned tee, choose a
spot in front of the ball
and aim over it rather
than at the target.

visualize the target, remember its position
as you look down at the ball, then aim
accurately toward it.

A square, parallel stance is not always
as easy to achieve as it sounds. Many
golfers find aiming an optical illusion and
simply cannot stand parallel to the line of
the shot without a great deal of care and
attention.

Check your alignment on the practice
ground by laying a club down along your
toes. You can do this on the course
providing that you only use the club you
are playing with and do not actually leave
it lying there as the shot is played.

Standing sideways to the target can be
difficult to judge. Generally the most
accurate way of lining up is to approach
the ball from behind, to choose a spot,
say, 18 inches ahead of the ball on line for
the target, to move round to the side of
the ball with this spot in mind, to aim the
clubface over this and to aim the feet
parallel to the imaginary line from the ball
to the spot.

(145)

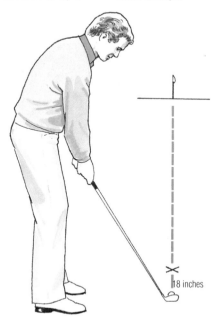

18 inches

REMEMBER
YOUR SWING
IS ONLY AS
ACCURATE AS
YOUR AIMING

FINESSE SHOTS

Good golf requires a repertoire of finesse shots. Some of these only come into use occasionally, but without them players can find themselves in situations with which they cannot cope.

The two shots illustrated opposite show you how to hook and slice the ball around trouble. The basic principle of each is to aim the stance and swing where you want the ball to start.

To hook the ball, strengthen the grip – with your left hand more on top and the right under – aim your feet well right of the obstacle and produce a flat, round-the-body swing through, closing the clubface

and tucking the left elbow in. Remember to start the ball to the right of the obstacle, over-allowing if anything, rather than under-allowing.

The slice is played by aiming the stance, shoulders and swing well left of the obstacle. Address the ball with the clubface open, your right hand a little more on the top of the grip and, if anything, tighter than normal.

Spin your hips sharply left through impact, holding the wrists stiff and the clubface open. The hip action starts the ball left, while the open clubface bends it away to the right.

A short shot from a shallow bunker often lends itself to putting or chipping the ball. In using either club – a putter or 7 iron – the depth of contact is crucial. With the putter, keep the ball above the sand and concentrate on a neat strike on the back of the ball. With the 7 iron, clip the sand as lightly as possible.

146

The good player can add a little wrist action to chipping. Keep the left wrist arched up, not dropped down. Any small amount of wrist action is limited by the end of the club just touching the inside of the left wrist. It does, however, add feel and finesse.

To hook around trouble, aim your stance and swing right and the clubface left. Strengthen the grip and produce a flat, round-the-body action. It is generally easier to get a large hook on the ball than to slice.

147

Slice around a tree by setting your stance and swing left, the clubface open and the right-hand grip tighter than normal. Watch out for extra height and keep well away from the branches.

REMEMBER
BEND A BALL
MORE WITH
HOOK THAN
SLICE

POSITIVE THINKING

When you stand for any golf shot, visualize the shot you want to play. The picture you have in your mind gives your brain and body a set of instructions to help you produce the correct technique. You have a built-in store of muscle memory on which to call.

Visualize a putt of a certain length and, with experience, your brain and body will automatically know what to do to achieve this. Much the same happens with pitching, bunker shots and right up through the long game.

What so easily happens, unfortunately, is that instead of thinking of the shot you want, you start thinking of the shot you are trying to avoid. Your thinking is along the lines of: "Please don't let me slice the ball away out of bounds."

The trouble is that now you have a picture of the ball slicing away out of bounds and your brain does not know that this is what you are trying to avoid. Your brain and body receive a set of instructions to slice the ball away out of bounds and this is what happens.

Concentrate on your tee shot ending up in the perfect position.

Eliminate memories of past mistakes.

In other words, if you think of the negative things you almost give yourself a set of instructions to carry them out. Think of dribbling the ball into a bunker in front of you and you will almost certainly do just that. Think of missing a putt to the left and the chances are that you will miss the putt to the left.

So think positively. Have a positive picture of the correct shot and never a negative picture of the wrong one.

You can help yourself think correctly around the golf course simply by sitting at home imagining the shots you are going to play. If you are having trouble with one particular par three, then imagine yourself playing the correct shot over and over again. Next time you are standing on the tee you have far more chance of producing the right picture and therefore encouraging the correct shot.

If you play a bad shot and keep repeating that bad shot over and over again, you will almost start giving yourself a set of instructions that makes things get worse.

Think of your putt
ending up in the hole.

149

Shut out of your mind the
problems that face you.

REMEMBER
THINK
POSITIVELY
AND PICTURE
EVERY SHOT

THE VALUE OF ROUTINE

Golf is a stationary ball game, which gives you time to adopt a routine for approaching each shot. But it also allows you too much time for thinking and therefore time for your mind to wander.

The value of repetition

Work at a routine in which you repeat the way in which you prepare for a shot. This encourages repetition in the golf swing itself. Learn to do the same thing on the practice ground as you do on the course and, in turn, learn to do the same thing on the course as you do in competition.

Lining up

As an example of routine, get used to leaving your bag and clubs in the same position to the right of the ball. Line up in the same way in practice and in play. Either walk up to the ball from the side or, preferably, go around behind the ball and line up from there, possibly over a spot in front of the ball. Do the same thing over and over again and do not be tempted to change it when you think the shot is especially difficult or important.

Looking up

Learn, too, to look up the same number of times. What easily happens is that you get on the practice ground, pull a ball forward and then look up once at the target before hitting it. You then get on the golf course and do something quite different, perhaps looking up several times before the hit. In a competitive situation, you possibly look up even more, move your feet or shuffle out of position, allowing time for indecision.

Posture

Set your posture in the same way each time, with your hands going on the club

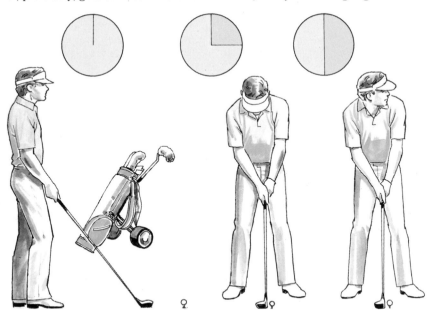

Top class players follow an exact pre-shot routine. You can almost set a stop-watch on them. Do the same. Always leave your clubs in a set position and line up the shot from behind ...

Take up your position, setting the feet and grip identically each time ...

Look up the same number of times – one, two or three – and "waggle" consistently ...

in the same manner, first the left, then the right and so on. Learn not to fiddle with your hands but get your grip on the club in two movements.

Waggles and twirls
Once you are addressing the ball, become repetitive with the number of waggles or twirls of the club you do. Don't let yourself suddenly waggle the club back and through half a dozen times in a competition if you do not do this in practice. Make the whole pre-shot routine as set as possible.

Watching the ball
Then learn to watch the ball well through impact and finish each swing with a perfectly balanced follow-through, holding it for a good four seconds. Even when you let the arms down, keep the legs balanced until the ball stops rolling. Watch the ball

Remember to watch the ball well through impact every time . . .

And produce a good finish . . .

to the end of its flight and roll, without losing balance and walking away from it.

If you watch good golfers, you will see that they do virtually the same each time they play the ball. You can almost set a stop-watch on many of them. Club golfers, by contrast, usually change their approach to shots and tend to lose the routine in a competition. As soon as they get anxious, they often slow down their preparation but, in contrast, actually speed up their swing.

Short game routine
Routine certainly does not stop when you get on to the short game. Use a definite routine when putting, as well. Read the green in the same way each time, have the same number of practice swings, keep your head still and aim for a repetitive stroke on every putting shot.

When you are suddenly faced with an important putt, don't feel that you need to do two or three extra practice swings. It achieves nothing. Do the same, however important the putt, as you would normally and you have every chance of repeating your successful action.

151

The finish
Remember that you can – and should – hold the finish. You do not have to run on after the ball or anything like that. You do not have to rush off to recover the ball to hit another shot. In this respect it is quite different from squash, football or tennis, for example.

Learn to repeat the swing and the whole routine from the moment you walk up to the ball to the time when you have finished the swing through. The more certain you are about the way you approach the shot, the more likely you are to repeat the swing itself and in turn enjoy better results.

REMEMBER
ADOPT A ROUTINE
AND ALWAYS
KEEP TO IT

LESSONS AND LEARNING

Your first two or three golf lessons can determine how your game develops. So always use a fully qualified professional and insist on taking a course of lessons – at least six and preferably ten. This gives your professional a chance to work systematically through the basic golfing techniques.

Lessons must be followed by practice. Aim for at least 250 balls' practice between lessons and don't expect to see any dramatic improvement without a combination of lessons and practice.

Do not be tempted to ask for too much information at each lesson. Good professionals will give you one or two key points to work on and perfect. Be patient.

Work methodically at each point in turn. It is all too easy, for example, to make the swing too complicated if you try to understand every aspect of it at once.

Keep a written note of what you learn and are working on. Remember that the same faults tend to creep in over and over again. Even experienced players often find basic problems arising with the grip or stance, for example, which recur right through their careers.

If possible, have your lessons videoed. The ideal method is for the professional to video you and comment audibly to give you a full record to study at home.

Make sure you have sessions on chipping, putting, pitching and bunker

shots. Players often ignore the short game, but this is where scoring can improve most quickly. Before you start your course, ask the professional to work on these aspects of the game, so that specific lessons can be prepared to coach you on these.

Try, too, to have the occasional playing lesson, so that your professional can see you in action on the course and work on strategy, aiming and general course management. Often players who aim well on the practice ground do something quite different on the course. So give your professional an opportunity to see this.

Once you are an established player, have lessons when you are playing *well*.

This gives the professional something to compare you with when things go wrong and makes it easier to pick out problems and help correct them.

Don't just go to the professional when you are desperate about your game and expect him to work miracles. To improve the swing, for example, can often mean producing worse shots before things get better. And results in terms of better scoring will take quite a few weeks of combined practice and play.

Stay with one professional, but bear in mind this word of warning. The professional who makes the swing seem complicated may not be giving you a swing that will work on the course.

Taking lessons with the aid of a video can be particularly helpful. You can see your own faults clearly, and since the camera does not lie, you really have to believe what you see. Even if the professional demonstrates your faults to you, there is no guarantee that he is mimicking your play exactly. With a video, you can take the film home and watch yourself. And make sure you get lessons on your short game, including bunker shots, as well as the long game.

153

REMEMBER
FOLLOW UP
LESSONS WITH
PRACTICE

LONG GAME PRACTICE

When practising your long game, always aim to a target, preferably a large one you might hit, such as an open umbrella. You will then have a reasonable chance of success and this will, in turn, boost your confidence. If you simply practise to a flag, the inevitable early failure will quickly get you down.

Set your target at the correct distance for each club and concentrate on every shot, trying to hit it to the best of your ability. Don't be careless.

Initially you will be working to improve your best shots. Good players then have to work at improving, then eliminating, bad shots. Always make an effort in practice to hit each shot well and try as hard as you would on the course.

Set yourself a programme for practice at the beginning of each session. For example:

● Play 20 shots with different clubs – 7 irons, 5 irons, fairway woods and drivers.
● Always start with irons and move on to woods.
● Don't hit too many balls at once. Start with 20 and then collect those – or have a short break before the next 20. If you hit too many, you are likely to become careless.

Once you can hit the ball reasonably well, begin to analyse your shots to pinpoint errors and to monitor improvements. Keep a record of your practice and check the results.

Note the grouping of the balls around your target. How many finish left and how many right? Are you achieving the distance you expect? How far do you hit the ball with each club, when you are using good golf balls?

For the beginner the grip is vital, so spend time practising it. Never pull balls forward without regripping the club. Take up the grip afresh for each shot until it feels simple and takes just a few seconds.

If you find it hard to go from practice to play, try varying the clubs, going from driver to iron to wood and so on. Take each club out of the bag in turn and really concentrate on each shot. This should help you adjust to each club you use on the course.

Practise lining up. Repeat your on-course routine, preferably lining up each from behind. *Never* hit shots without lining up. Don't just put a club down along your toes for lining up. You cannot keep it there during play.

Where possible, use three piles of balls a few yards apart and move from one to another so that your lining up has to be absolutely accurate for each shot.

Think of a round of golf as, for example, 14 drives, four par threes, eight fairway woods, 10 medium or long irons, 10 short irons and so on. Practise in set batches from each kind of shot.

Generally practise from reasonable lies to get into the groove for a good swing. But also practise occasional shots from bad lies with sloping stances.

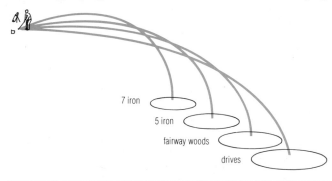

7 iron

5 iron

fairway woods

drives

A useful programme for practising long shots **(left)** is to play, say, 20 balls with different clubs. Start with a 7 iron, then a 5 iron, then a fairway wood and finally a driver. Check the distances for each.

Even the great players like Greg Norman **(right)** have to practise and take their game very seriously.

155

REMEMBER
PRACTISE TO
GET IN
THE SWING

SHORT GAME PRACTICE

As a rule, the easiest way to improve your scoring is through practising the short game. Higher handicap players often waste needless shots around the green. Time spent practising your short game will always pay off. Improving full shots usually takes much longer.

With short pitching, practise 10 to 20 yard shots with a sand wedge to an upturned umbrella. Listen for the ball to land in it. Then practise pitching over a golf bag or another club to represent a bunker. Practise from good lies and then from tight and poor lies.

To practise chipping, use 5 balls and aim to hole each. Score 5 points for holing out, 3 if within clubhead-to-grip length and 1 within a club-length.

Combine short pitching, chipping and putting. Play 10 shots from off the green and count how many you get down in two. Good players can try the same exercise with short bunker shots. Practise up and down banks to get used to different situations.

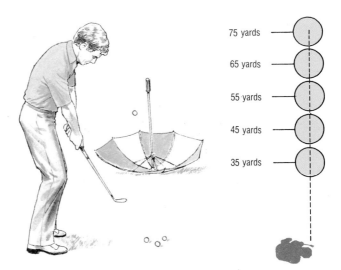

Practise putting and short 7-iron chipping at home on a smooth carpet **(above right)**. Aim at a matchbox or into a glass — something smaller than a golf hole — from various distances.

Practise short pitching into an umbrella and long pitching to a set of hoops or umbrellas at varying, measured distances **(right)**. Get a feel for the distances to give yourself a guide on the course.

75 yards

65 yards

55 yards

45 yards

35 yards

Always practise with a definite plan and monitor your improvement. Take time with your short shots, which all require firm wrists – never loose and sloppy. Remember – loose for long shots and stiff for short shots.

As a general rule for all short shots, the backswing and throughswing mirror each other for length – *never* long back and decelerating.

A good short game routine is to practise with a clubhead cover trapped between your right elbow and your body. This keeps the left arm working correctly, with arms, legs and body in harmony to keep the cover in place.

Most short shots (right) require a shortish backswing and acceleration through the ball. Practise with a partner holding another club behind you to limit the backswing. Make the two halves of the swing mirror each other.

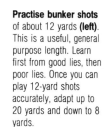

Practise bunker shots of about 12 yards **(left)**. This is a useful, general purpose length. Learn first from good lies, then poor lies. Once you can play 12-yard shots accurately, adapt up to 20 yards and down to 8 yards.

REMEMBER
PRACTISE THE SHORT GAME TO LOWER SCORES

BALL CONTROL

The essence of good golf is to hit the ball repeatedly to a target. A good swing on its own does not do this, so you need to be target orientated. Aim for a target and hit it, both in practice and in play. When you are playing a friendly game, nominate the target you intend to hit and the shot you want to play.

Think positively of the target you have chosen and not the obstacles you are trying to avoid. With every shot, make

With all shots make your key thought to hit the ball to a target, either where it will land or where it will finish. Keep the target in mind.

hitting the target your key thought and keep this firmly in your mind.

Many great golfers start playing with just one or two clubs. Lee Trevino and Seve Ballesteros, for example, both started life as caddies using just one club and had to do everything with it. They learnt to play all sorts of shots by opening or closing the clubface and adapting the swing as necessary.

Other professionals make a point of practising with a limited number of clubs to produce feel, touch and ball control.

Do not be obsessed with the swing: be obsessed with hitting the target.

Try to produce a whole range of shots with any one club. Start with a 7 iron and then a 4 iron. Practise a full range of shots for all distances, from 5 yards to a full shot, hitting the ball high, low, out to the right and hooked to the left.

To get the feeling of really good ball control, the aspiring tournament player should be able to manoeuvre the ball from 50 yards upward with a 5 wood and driver. Obviously these are not the type of shots you would ever use, but you should develop an awareness of the clubhead and a feel for the clubface.

Learn to relate spin in golf to that in other ball games. A slice is like a cut shot in tennis or table tennis. The wrists are

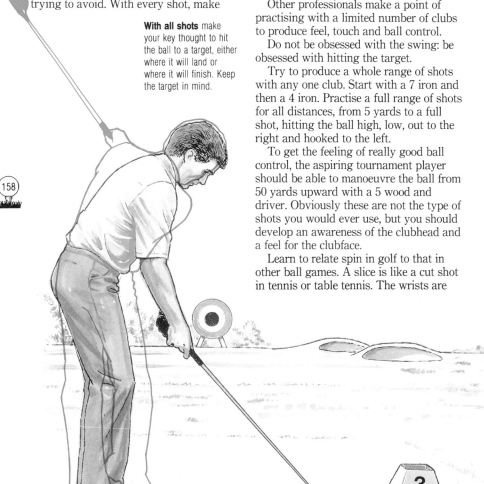

158

3

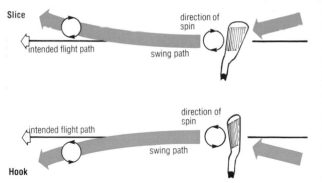

SPINNING THE BALL

Aim at being able to spin the ball both ways. If you know how to put spin on the ball, you are more able to take off unwanted sidespin and straighten out any faults.

If you can spin the ball it will help you with a variety of shots.

Slice

intended flight path

direction of spin

swing path

direction of spin

intended flight path

swing path

Hook

held firm and the head of the weapon held back and open – and you use a cut-across action to drop and stop the shot.

With tennis, the ball pulls up quickly – as it will with a fade or slice in golf. To cut the tennis ball, you lift the racket and chop across the ball. You should have just the same feeling in golf. If you prefer, relate this to kicking a football, with the foot held "open" to create a glancing blow.

To produce the draw or hook shot, you should get more of a feeling of creating topspin. Imagine the spin from right to left, trying to put a glancing blow on the ball in the other direction. Instead of holding the wrists back stiffly, let them loosen, with your arms and wrists rolling over to close the clubface as necessary.

159

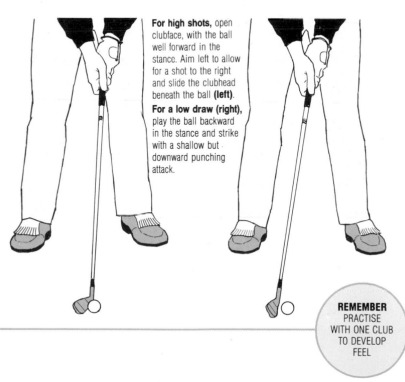

For high shots, open clubface, with the ball well forward in the stance. Aim left to allow for a shot to the right and slide the clubhead beneath the ball **(left)**.

For a low draw (right), play the ball backward in the stance and strike with a shallow but downward punching attack.

REMEMBER
PRACTISE
WITH ONE CLUB
TO DEVELOP
FEEL

CURING THE SLICE

The slice, in which the ball bends away to the right, is a problem for probably 75 percent of golfers. It is a stiff-wristed shot which cut the ball away to the right.

The bend becomes more noticeable with the driver, which creates far more sidespin than the lofted clubs. In fact, players tend to pull iron shots left and slice wood shots right.

Slicing is caused by leaving the clubface open – aiming right – at impact, either from a weak grip or stiffness in the wrists through impact. In trying to correct this, players aim their feet left and swing across the ball toward the left. This adds

swing path
out to in

target path

open face

swing path
in to out

The typical slicer's action – hands too far ahead of the ball through impact and clubface wide open. At first players may slice simply by leaving the clubface open. They then start aiming and swinging left to counteract this, but in doing so create more sidespin.

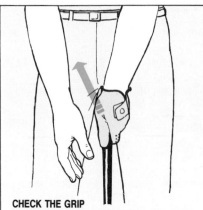

CHECK THE GRIP
The grip is very important. Any tendency for the
Vs to point to the chin will produce an open
clubface. Keep the left hand well on top, the right
under the club, with the Vs to the right shoulder.
The interlocking grip can be too tight. Try the
Vardon or baseball grip instead and look for
looseness in the hands and wrists.

more sidespin and the slice gets worse.
The more they try to keep the ball left, the
farther right it bends.

You must correct the slice firstly by
eliminating sidespin and secondly by
correcting the direction of the swing.
Check your grip. The line between the
thumb and index finger of both hands
should point to the right shoulder or even
outside it. Keep the left arm loose beyond
impact and let it fold out of the way, with
the elbow folding in and not breaking out.

Try to close the clubface and hook the
ball. Let it go as far left as you like,
rolling the arms and wrists over if
necessary in order to feel the opposite
spin to the slice.

Be "afraid" of the left side of the course,
rather than the right. Once you start
pulling shots to the left, it is logical to
correct the out-to-in (left-aimed) swing. At
this point ensure the stance is square,
from feet to shoulders, with the right
shoulder down and relaxed.

**Once you have
eliminated the slice
spin,** try to correct the
swing path, always taking
the club back in a
shallow curve. Think
"wide, inside". Swing the
club back behind you as
you would a racket.

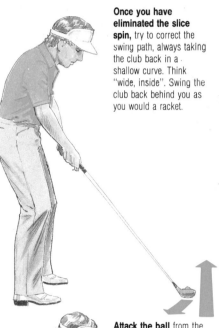

Attack the ball from the
inside, in other words on
the same curve as the
backswing. Turn well into
the backswing, getting
your back facing the
target. And resist
applying force with the
right shoulder. Feel you
are keeping it still and
swing your left arm and
club away from it into
impact.

(161)

REMEMBER
STIFF = SLICE
LOOSE = LEFT

THE BEGINNER'S BAD SHOTS

Most beginners suffer from bad shots caused not so much by bad swinging as poor contact. The clubhead is small, the ball is small and the ground tends to get in the way of the swing. It takes practice and a perfect eye to strike the ball correctly.

Learn how to correct poor contact – topped shots, fluffed shots and shots from the toe or socket (heel) of the club. You can do a great deal to improve your strike simply by concentrating on contact, watching the ball and keeping good balance throughout.

Topped shots

These are the most common fault, in which the ball runs low along the ground. To get it airborne, you must find the bottom of the ball. If the clubhead brushes the ground, the loft will get the ball up. Topping usually results from trying to lift the ball and bringing up the clubhead. This is made worse if you look at the top of the ball and not the back.

Topping can also result from tension – breathing in and lifting your body. Be wary, too, of keeping your head low down at address, since it is then forced to lift through impact, with the clubhead.

With irons, keep the ball central in the stance and hit *down* through the ball with a divot, moving your weight on to the left foot through impact. With drivers, aim to hit the tee peg out of the ground. The ball will then rise as desired.

Fluffed shots

The clubhead catches the ground first. This is caused by loosening the grip at the top of the backswing, decelerating into impact and having the ball too far forward at address.

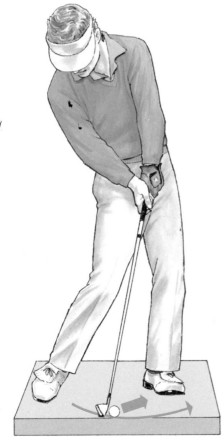

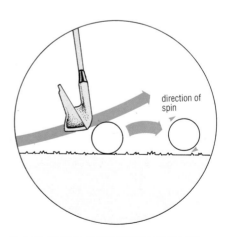

direction of spin

If you try to lift the ball the clubhead will rise and catch the top **(above)**. Transfer your weight to the left foot through impact. Hit down through the ball with a divot to force the ball up **(left)**.

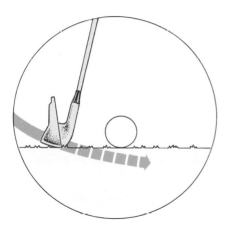

Toe or socket shots

A ball hit with the toe or socket will fly sharply off to the right. With the toe you may be too far from the ball at address and pulling your arms in through impact. With the socket, you may be too near at address or too far away and toppling forward on impact. Watch the ball and *balance* at the finish.

In the socket shot (below), the ball flies away to the right.

163

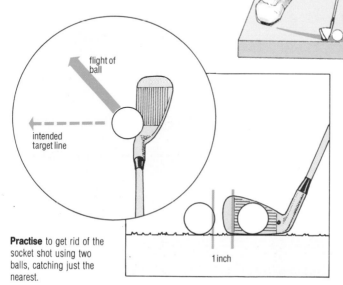

flight of ball

intended target line

Practise to get rid of the socket shot using two balls, catching just the nearest.

1 inch

With fluffed shots the club hits the ground behind the ball **(above left)**. Keep the ball fairly central in the stance, with hands firm enough to control the club, and aim for a ball then divot contact, with your weight on the left heel through impact **(above)**.

REMEMBER
THINK OF AND LISTEN FOR A GOOD CONTACT

THE PUSH AND HOOK

The push and hook are faults often found in good players. Both shots start out to the right of the target, but the push then goes straight on to the right and the hook bends quite sharply back to the left.

To correct a push, first check your aiming. If you are doing this correctly, with your feet parallel to the shot, you are likely to push shots because you are:

● Playing the ball too far back in the stance.

● Swaying to the left through impact.

● Trying for an exaggerated in-to-out attack.

● Adopting a blocked leg action, with your hips to the right of the target in the finish.

● Turning your right foot too far out at address and inhibiting the throughswing.

A true hook starts out to the right in just the same way as the push, so look for the same causes here. It then spins back to the left through a closed clubface. A true hook, starting right from a square stance, is quite unusual and is a fault of the good player.

To correct it, check the grip, bringing the Vs nearer the chin, clear the hips and legs through to face the target and swing the arms and club up – and not around – beyond impact.

Most club golfers who think they hook usually have a pull hook. This is not caused by an in-to-out attack, as are the push and hook. The cause here is almost always a bad grip, with the left hand positioned too far over and the right placed too far under.

Such golfers close the clubface at impact, often with the right hand and shoulder dominating the movement. The ball is pulled and bends to the left. They then offset this by aiming their feet to the right.

You can correct this action by checking the grip – with the Vs pointing nearer to the chin than the right shoulder. Also work at swinging with the left hand to strengthen it. This should produce shots pushed away to the right. Then correct the alignment.

hook   push

The push and hook
both start to the right
from a square stance.
With a pushed shot the
ball flies straight right.
With a hook it bends
back to the left because
of the closed clubface.

164

**Correct a push or hook
(left)**, by learning to clear
the hips and legs through
to face the target in the
finish.

Correct a ball bending
to the left by checking
the Vs in the grip
(below). With a hooker's
grip, the Vs point outside
the right shoulder. Adjust
the grip and experiment
with the Vs pointing
nearer the chin.

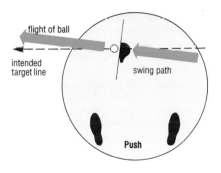

flight of ball

intended
target line

swing path

Push

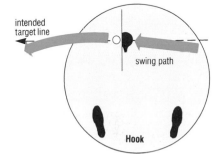

intended
target line

swing path

Hook

165

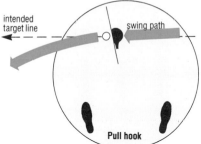

intended
target line

swing path

Pull hook

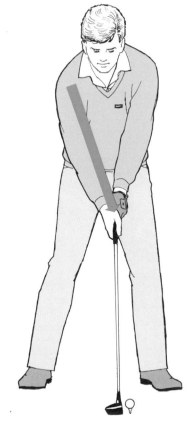

A push (top), is caused
by an in-to-out swing,
with the clubface square
to the swing path.

A hook (centre), is
caused by an in-to-out
swing from a square
stance, with the clubface
more or less square to
the target.

Do not confuse a pull
hook with a hook. In a
pull hook **(above)**,
players often have an
out-to-in swing and a
poor grip which closes
the clubface. They then
aim off to the right to
counteract this.

REMEMBER
FINISH
FACING
THE TARGET

HITTING IT FARTHER

Long hitting is achieved by striking the ball cleanly from the middle of the clubface, with clubhead speed rather than force. To generate clubhead speed, feel loose with the driver at address and make sure that there is freedom in your wrists. Turn fully in the backswing, allowing time for the change of direction at the top. Keep your wrists loose and free and work to a full balanced finish.

The balance and follow-through are vital. Players who give the impression of swinging too fast are usually guilty of poor balance. You should finish well on the left heel and toes of the right foot. Make sure that your wrists are free and

One of the keys to a long hitting is *balance*. Hit through the ball to a full follow-through that is controlled. Aim for a finish with the clubshaft on to your left shoulder, balancing on your left foot and the toes of the right. A positive, attacking attitude will bring rewards of length.

get the clubshaft through on to the left shoulder or back of the neck.

It is also necessary to strike the ball with a square clubface or a slightly closing one. This will enable you to achieve maximum carry and will also add run to your shots.

Players who lose length often strike the ball with an open clubface, producing a high cutting shot that stops the ball dead on landing. This is often the result of a steep chopping action, stiff wrists and too much force from the shoulders instead of speed in the arms and hands.

Think positively about length. Do not be tentative. Choose a definite target, visualize it and then attack it. Don't try to steer the ball straight. Let fly at it with uninhibited freedom.

Bear in mind that a well-timed shot often goes farther than one in which you try to give it everything.

Distance comes from clubhead speed, not force. Aim for good clubhead speed by striking from the middle of the clubface **(below)**, which should be square or slightly closing, and a clean shallow attack.

The wrists need to be loose and free through impact to develop length. Only firm them up once you can hit like a professional and hook rather than slice. Let your left arm turn and fold away beyond impact.

167

PERCENTAGE GOLF: 1

Playing percentage golf means thinking particularly about the options for each shot – weighing up the possibility of success and failure – and the consequences of various types of shot.

Even the top professional golfer is not going to play perfect shots all the time. Ben Hogan, one of golf's perfectionists, suggested he might hope for two or three perfect shots a round.

Percentage golf means that you always allow for a realistic margin of error – depending on your ability – and, while thinking positively, choose a shot that gives you a margin for the less than perfect shot.

The example illustrated below shows a typical recovery situation where you need to apply the principles of percentage golf. Some choices are probably wrong, others *definitely* wrong and others correct. It is helpful to analyse the thinking behind each selection.

The overall objective is to find a spot for the next shot with a good lie, a flat stance, an open line to the green and close enough to reach the green. You may have to sacrifice distance for the sake of safety.

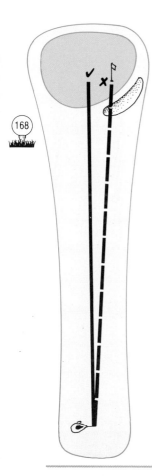

An example of good thinking (left). Why take the risky shot over the bunker? You may land in it. If not, you will probably be too bold and finish at the back of the green. You can aim safely clear of the green and probably get far closer, with little risk.

A typical recovery situation (right), with various choices to make, some good and some bad. Recovery shots are not usually hard to execute, but need clear, logical thinking. Numbers **1** to **5** represent the wrong choices and letters **A** to **C** the correct ones:
1 Straight-out safety. This is too cautious because you cannot reach the green.
A This shot is just as safe and close enough to make the green.
2 This looks all right, but has gone marginally too far, leaving a shot over the bunkers. It would be worse, of

course, to leave the ball short of **A** and be blocked by the large tree.
3 This is definitely too far, in the rough and behind the three conifers.
4 This has worked out all right, but going over or through the trees is very risky and here unnecessary, compared with **B**.
B This shot makes up some length, with less risk.
C This is a very sensible route on to the next fairway, giving you a good lie and a clear shot to the green. It is probably better than shot **5**.
5 Here you risked catching the tree branches and the rough and leaving a tricky shot over the bunker.

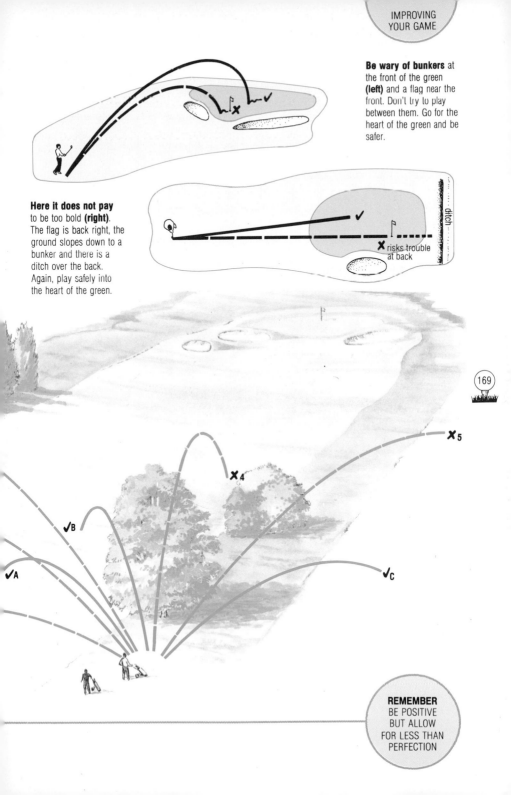

Be wary of bunkers at the front of the green **(left)** and a flag near the front. Don't try to play between them. Go for the heart of the green and be safer.

Here it does not pay to be too bold **(right)**. The flag is back right, the ground slopes down to a bunker and there is a ditch over the back. Again, play safely into the heart of the green.

ditch

✗ risks trouble
at back

169

✗5

✗4

✓B

✓A

✓C

REMEMBER
BE POSITIVE
BUT ALLOW
FOR LESS THAN
PERFECTION

PERCENTAGE GOLF: 2

Shots around the green require clear thinking and good decision making. Typically they require you to negotiate banks, rough or a bunker. You need to play a shot that, if possible, does not demand absolute perfection.

Don't try to pitch a ball 3 feet over a bunker or run it to within 6 inches of the bunker and be disappointed when you finish up in it.

Look for a slightly safer route, allowing for slight errors and thinking positively about the chosen shot.

Take a typical situation from the fairway, in which you have to play over a bunker, with a bank over that, and with the flag fairly close to it.

Don't aim to land on the top of the bunker, if there is a flat surface by the flag. If you drop it on the downslope, it will run through. Land on the flat and the ball will stop.

Look at the shot from the side to assess the slope and be realistic about the landing space. Avoid landing on downslopes.

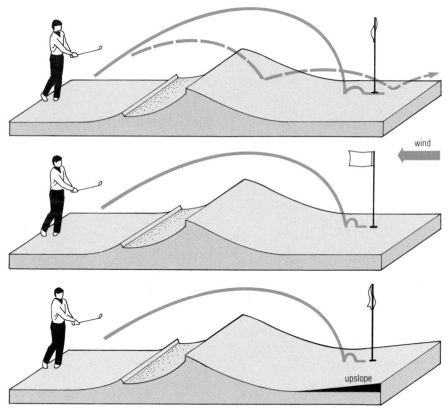

170

wind

upslope

Landing on the downslope (top) is far riskier than necessary. Land on the flat and the ball will stop. If playing into the wind **(centre)**, be bold. The ball can be pitched all the way and will stop. When playing over a bunker **(above)**, where the flag is on an upslope, aim to leave yourself an uphill putt. With the wind **(above right)**, and on a downhill slope, a short pitch to the side allows the ball room to roll.

Professionals do not always aim at the centre of the fairway or at the flag. They are prepared to zig-zag to avoid trouble off the tee.

Equally they will not always aim at the flag with approach shots or when pitching. Sometimes the sideways route is preferable and safer.

It may be better to get 12 feet from the hole to the side than 6 feet short or past it, if the slopes are tricky.

When the wind is blowing from behind you, or there is a downslope to the flag, stopping the ball can be a problem. Think of going to the side of a bunker or bank, which allows you to pitch the ball shorter, giving it more room to roll.

Perhaps in the situation shown below you might have a slope from the right, which will help the ball back down to the hole and will add to the advantage of playing safe.

Look, too, for the slightly sideways line if playing from a poor lie. A running shot to the side may be simpler than the pitch shot over the bunker.

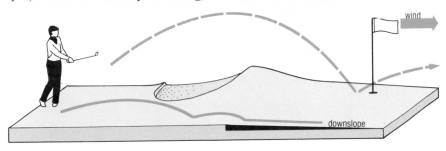

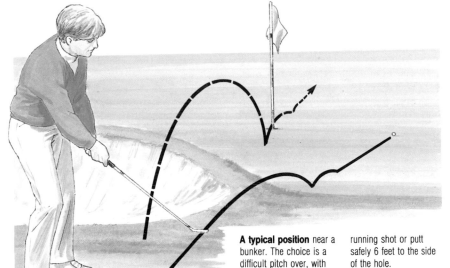

A typical position near a bunker. The choice is a difficult pitch over, with little or no chance of stopping by the flag, *or* a running shot or putt safely 6 feet to the side of the hole.

REMEMBER
BE PREPARED
TO ZIG-ZAG
AWAY FROM
TROUBLE

171

READING THE COURSE: 1

When you are faced with playing a course for the very first time, what is the best way to approach it and how do you work out what shots to play? The example here and over the page is of a special nine holes, which together incorporate a whole range of situations you are likely to come across on any golf course. Advice and warnings are offered on the shots you can try at each of the holes.

1 Par five 485 yards Dog-leg
The correct drive here is well left of centre to give you a clear shot around the corner. Tee up on the right side to help aim away from trouble on the right. The next shot is important. Get enough length to be clear of the trees on the right, preferably far enough to reach the green for three. With this kind of hole, watch for the danger of hitting too far with the second shot and being caught by another tree, bunker or thick rough.

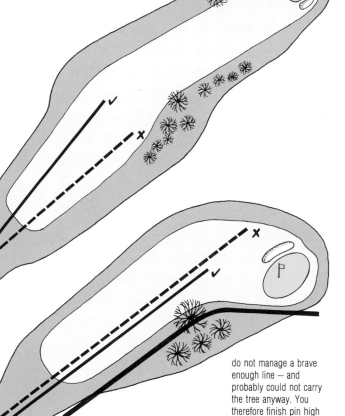

2 Par four 285 yards Short dog-leg
You are tempted to try to reach the green. The large tree and ditch to the right make the drive at the green risky. You do not manage a brave enough line — and probably could not carry the tree anyway. You therefore finish pin high left, with a tricky shot over the bunker. It is far safer to play a shorter tee shot into position, leaving a simple shot at the flag. Try to check the pin position when playing another hole.

**3 Par four 330 yards
Offset green**
Watch for this on a short par 4. The correct drive is well down the right side, into light rough on the right if necessary. From here you have a clear shot at the flag along the green. A drive in the centre of the fairway is not ideal. Here the second shot is more difficult. Look at the flag position from the tee to work out the ideal drive. If you cannot see it, check the green if you pass it playing another hole.

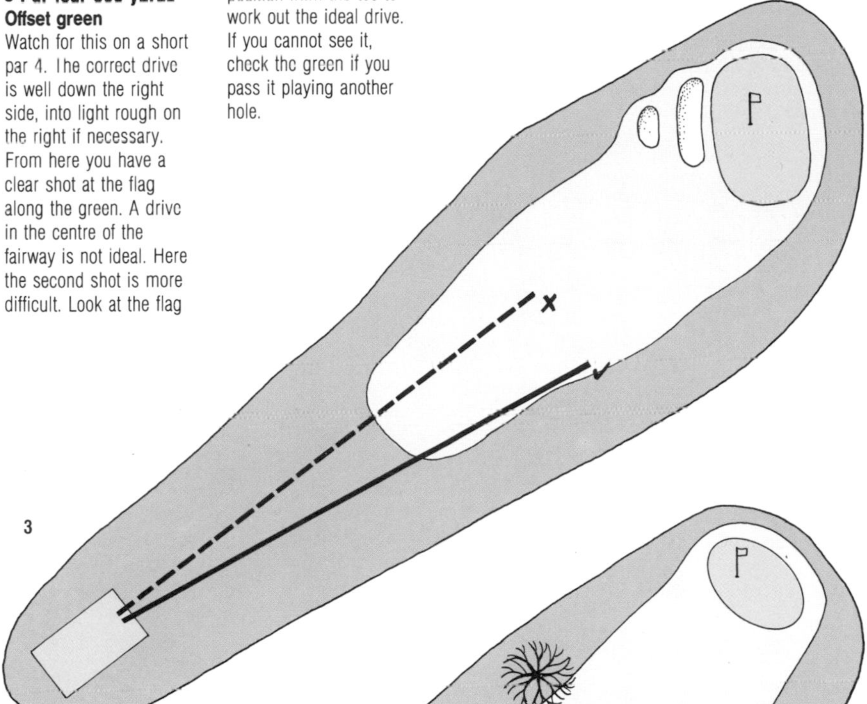

3

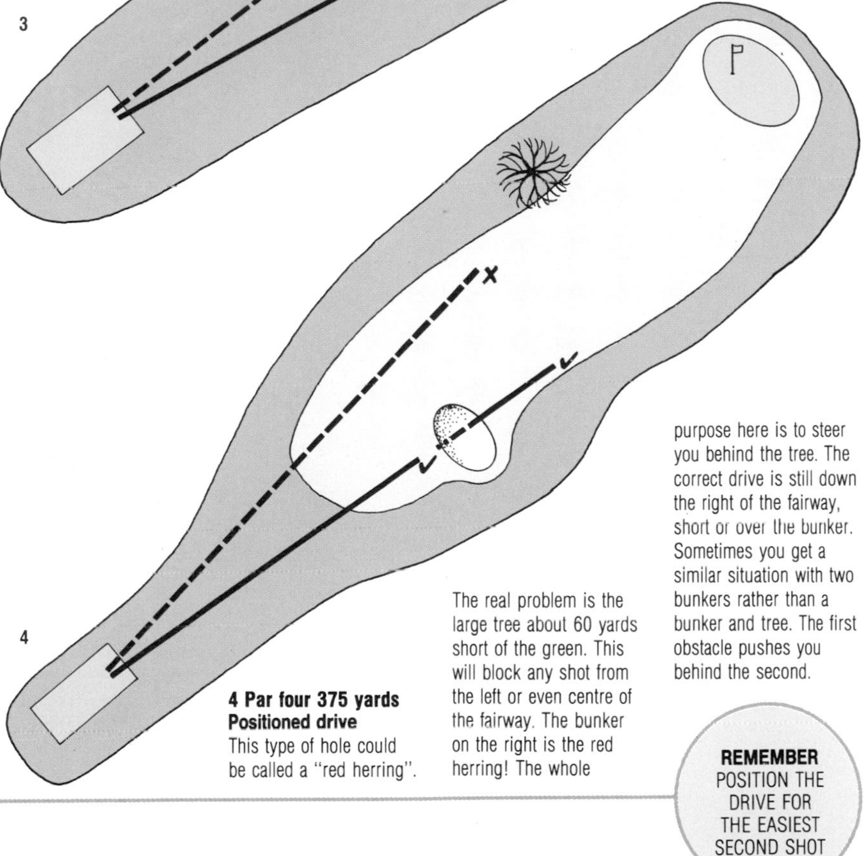

173

4

**4 Par four 375 yards
Positioned drive**
This type of hole could be called a "red herring".

The real problem is the large tree about 60 yards short of the green. This will block any shot from the left or even centre of the fairway. The bunker on the right is the red herring! The whole purpose here is to steer you behind the tree. The correct drive is still down the right of the fairway, short or over the bunker. Sometimes you get a similar situation with two bunkers rather than a bunker and tree. The first obstacle pushes you behind the second.

REMEMBER
POSITION THE
DRIVE FOR
THE EASIEST
SECOND SHOT

READING THE COURSE: 2

5 Par five 520 yards
Indecision
The planning behind this hole is to create a bunker at the exact distance for the second shot. On this par 5 the bunker is right in the way of a full second shot, perhaps 100 yards short of the green. You are not quite certain whether you can carry it. Then you cannot decide whether to play short, go right or go left! Faced with indecision, you are likely to play a poor shot. So, with an obstacle like this, make a definite choice and be committed to it.

5

6

6 Par four 295 yards
Two-tier green
Watch for the short par 4 with a two-tier plateau green, particularly if the green is small. A plateau green often drains well and the ball pitching on it will not hold. If playing to the upper layer of a two-tier green, aim to be able to run the ball up on to the top layer. The shortness of the hole may tempt you to hit wildly off the tee. Instead, make certain the tee shot is accurate, giving yourself a clear run at the green without having to pitch over bunkers.

7

7 Par four 410 yards
Cross bunkers
You are faced with the choice of going for the carry or playing short. On your own course, make sure you establish a definite landmark from where you know you can make the carry. Also weigh up the odds of a successful recovery on to the green if you do go in. If you make the carry and still cannot reach the green, don't bother. If the bunker is shallow or fairly close to the green, the gamble may be worth taking. Knowing exact distances helps if you do play short.

8 Par five 485 yards
Sloping fairway

With a hole that slopes from left to right, your shots will all tend to slice to the right in the air. The ball will also tend to kick to the right on landing. Aim sufficiently far left, always keeping above the green and on the higher side of the fairway. Beware of bunkers and trees on the right side of the fairway.

175

9 Par four 340 yards
Irresistible carry

Beware of the large bunkers or pond just short of your driving distance, which seems a tempting obstacle to carry. Sometimes, particularly on a course you do not know, you cannot resist the challenge of trying to carry it. First ask yourself if you will gain anything by carrying it. Secondly, be alert for another hazard, perhaps out of sight from the tee, beyond it. It is there to tempt you to have a go!

REMEMBER
IDENTIFY ALL
THE HAZARDS

EXERCISES: 1

Good golfers need flexibility and strength. Although many do not do any form of physical training as such, they are usually far more flexible and mobile that one would think, with a high degree of fitness. These physical assets can be improved by a regular work-out that concentrates on those areas related to the game of golf.

Staying loose

When you think about the end of the swing, your left foot stays pointing out in front of you while your hips turn at a right angle to this. If you do not have reasonable looseness in the ankles, you will restrict the follow-through. And your back and waist need to be loose in order to turn and pivot in the backswing.

The left arm needs to be able to work freely from the left shoulder in order to swing across the chest. Arms and shoulders must not feel as though they work as one in the golf swing. It should be very much the feeling of swinging the arms to the right shoulder, away from it and to the left shoulder. The left arm, in particular, needs looseness. Make sure, too, that your hands and wrists are loose in order to generate clubhead speed. And your neck needs to be loose to allow the head to stay still and the body to move.

The following are some loosening exercises to use before any round of golf. They include all the parts of the body you will need to strengthen and keep supple, working from the neck downward.

Head and neck
Start from the top by holding your head up and then tipping it to the right, as though touching your right shoulder with your right ear, and then to the left. Get rid of all the creaks and groans, taking it slowly and just feeling the neck stretching.

Finger loosening
Now move down to the fingers. Hold your hands out in front of you, palms of the hands downward. Stretch the fingers out in front, keeping them together. Start with finger splits to get them working and get the hands coordinated.

Firstly, split the fingers, keeping the

inside two together and working the outside two apart. Keep doing this repeatedly and then split them the other way. Now work at the first and second fingers together, and the third and fourth fingers together. Split them apart, draw them together again, split them apart, draw them together.

Wrist work
Next move on to the wrists and get those working. Shake them just to get them feeling loose and to encourage the feeling of a throwing action. Imagine you are holding a clinical thermometer and trying to shake the mercury down into the bulb.

Having got the wrists generally loose, try pulling the thumbs back on to your forearms, gradually increasing the angle you can achieve. With your wrists, you should look for

movement in four directions. You should get a roughly 90-degree movement in the direction of the palm.

By hingeing the wrist back, you should again achieve a good 90-degree movement. Hinge the wrist over toward the thumb; here you should look for a movement of, say, 30 degrees. Hinge it over toward the little finger; the movement should be about 45 degrees. Work at loosening both wrists in all four directions for increased mobility.

The right wrist
Particularly important for
the golfer is to be able to
get the right wrist back
on itself to a good right
angle. If you cannot do
this, hold the right hand
out in front of you, with
the palm against the wall
and arms straight. Start
with the hand out at
shoulder width and then
gradually work the hand
inch by inch down the
wall until you achieve a
slightly larger angle.
Never force the
movement.

Left arm loosening
You need freedom to
work the left arm across
the chest toward the right
shoulder. Hold both arms
out straight in front of
you at shoulder height.
Put your right hand
beside your left elbow
and just draw the left arm

across the chest, keeping
it straight, until it touches
the right shoulder. With
the palm of the hand
down, this is exactly the
sort of movement you
should get in the
backswing. This also
loosens up the back of
the shoulder.

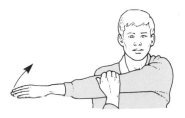

Toe touching
Move on to the simple
exercise of touching your
toes. The feeling here is
of bending from the hips,
just the same bend as
you need in the posture
for the golf swing. If you
can touch your toes
easily, try the same
standing on the bottom
step of a flight of stairs
and aim to get the tips of
your fingers down below
the level of your feet.

Trunk bends
Work, too, at sideways
trunk bends. Stand with
your feet apart and hold
your arms out to the
sides. Now bend over to
the right and try to ease
your right hand down
your right leg as far as
you can. Don't bounce it
up and down; just ease it
down gradually. Then
stand upright and bend
over to the left, again

easing the left hand and
left fingertips down the
left leg. Move from side
to side, taking things
slowly and definitely
without any bouncing
action.

EXERCISES: 2

Ham string stretch
Now move on to the legs and stretch the ham strings. Put your right foot out in front of you and squat down with hands on your right knee. Put the left leg out straight behind you, with

the left foot straight in front, forming the straight line along the left foot and the right foot. Simply press down on the right knee with your hands and remain in this completely stationary position.

You should feel this gently stretching the ham strings of the left leg. There is no bouncing; it is static. Now repeat the same exercise with the right leg out behind you.

Shoulder loosening
Lastly, loosen up the shoulders. Take hold of a driver, with one hand at one end of the club and the other at the other end. Hold the club up above you and swing it down in front of you and then back over your head, keeping your arms

straight. Gradually work at drawing the hands closer together until you can do the same with one of the shorter clubs such as a wedge.
Don't do this just before going out to play golf, however. Use it as a general purpose loosening exercise.

178

Hands, arms and wrists
Good golf depends on having strong hands and arms. One of the difficulties with the game is that it requires the left and right hands and arms to be of almost equal strength. Most right-handed players find that they need to do some exercising of the left hand for it to work properly during the swing. The following are some ideas on general hand and wrist strengthening.

Finger strengthening
One of the best and easiest of exercises is simply to squeeze a rubber ball and work it around in the fingers. This gives mobility to the

fingers and also builds up general strength. Again work with both right and left hands and don't ignore the little fingers, particularly with the left hand.

Forearms and fingers

Another good exericse, which seems very simple, but which strengthens forearms and fingers, is to do finger stretches at arm's length. Hold your arms straight out at shoulder height, with the fingers stretched out wide in front of you. Draw them In and push them out again – in, out, in, out – as fast and strongly as possible. At first this exercise scems innocuous. But as you build up the numbers, you will gradually find the forearms feeling some resistance, while exercising the whole hand through to the fingertips.

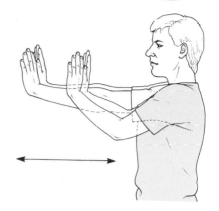

Strengthening the arms

One of the most widely advocated exercises for golfers is to attach a weight on the end of a piece of string to something like a broom handle, then hold this out at arm's length and wind the weight up and down.

Try tying a practice ball bag with a piece of rope on to a broom handle or old golf clubshaft. You can then fill the bag with an increasing number of balls to make the exercise more difficult.

Arms and clubhead control

Another simple exercise, which again has more effect than you would think, is to hold a golf club at arm's length and to write your name in the air with the clubhead. This not only exercises the arms of those who are not naturally strong, but also teaches a degree of clubhead control.

Wrist twists

For those who may have access to dumb-bells, there are two excellent exercises using wrist twists. First, hold the dumb-bells with your elbows into the side and rotate them – in, out, in, out. This puts emphasis on strengthening the upper arms. Then do the same with the elbows supported on a table. This will now exercise the lower arm while increasing wrist mobility.

The choice of weights for the dumb-bells is important – it is essential to use a weight that will strengthen the arms but which is not too heavy to repeat the exercise up to 40 times.

REMEMBER
KEEP SUPPLE
TO SWING
SUCCESSFULLY

EXERCISES: 3

Exercising with a club
Good golfers have to be strong in both the left and right hands. One useful exercise for any serious golfer is to swing the club with your left arm. Use a medium iron, gripping it as normal with the left hand, but

possibly with the left thumb slightly more down the front than usual.

Swing the club up to the top of the backswing, supporting it on the left thumb, and then swing it on through, letting the left elbow bend to a right

angle, with the clubshaft resting across your back. It is important that the left arm is allowed to bend as it goes on through. Then return the club slowly to the address and keep repeating this.

Don't just swing back

and through with a continuous movement, since this achieves nothing. Also guard against keeping the left arm straight beyond impact. This is not what should happen in the golf swing.

Improving the backswing
Another strengthening exercise is to swing the club up to the top of the backswing with just the left arm, from there holding firmly with the left wrist and twisting the wrist over and back, over and back, so that it flattens or arches over in one direction and then returns back into a flat or slightly cupped position. This begins to work the muscles of the left wrist and will eventually help you to achieve a good backswing position.

Hands, wrists and forearms
An excellent exercise, and quite a simple one, is to swish one of the medium irons back and through in long rough grass. Keep the swing short and punchy to strengthen your hands, wrists and forearms.

Exercising the legs and back

Possibly the best leg exercise of all – and one used by Seve Ballesteros and Nick Faldo, for example – is cycling. Many professional golfers use it as a form of winter training, either on a bicycle or a cycling machine if the weather does not allow outdoor work.

Leg pushes
Your legs need to be strong for golf. A simple exercise, needing no extra equipment, is to stand with one foot on a firm upright chair and to push up on that leg. With the leg straight, lower yourself slowly until you touch the ground again. Keep repeating this, slowly up and down, then reverse the movement, trying it on the other leg. It takes little time and tones up the whole of both legs.

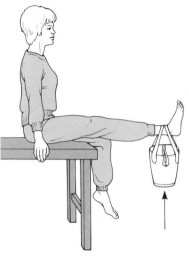

Leg lifts
Another popular leg strengthening exercise for golfers is to sit on a table with a practice ball bag suspended over one ankle. Simply lift and lower the bag, gradually increasing the number of lifts and also increasing the number of balls in the bag.

Wall sits
A good exercise for the upper legs. Try sitting against a wall, where you simply slide your back down it, with your upper legs out horizontally in front of you. At first this seems extremely straightforward, but after a few minutes soon becomes punishing on the upper legs and does a good deal to strengthen them.

181

REMEMBER
DEVELOP
STRENGTH
IN BOTH
HANDS

EXERCISES: 4

Squat thrusts and burpees

Two other energetic leg-up exercises are squat thrusts and burpees. The first is a well-known exercise, bending over with your hands on the floor and feet almost between your hands, pushing your legs and feet out behind you and then drawing them in in front of you. Burpees are a combination of a squat thrust with a jump added. Out with the feet, in with the feet. Stand up, jump, stretch, down again and repeat the action.

Skipping

As a general and leg exercise, there is little to beat skipping.

Leg raises

To exercise the back and legs, lie down on your back and raise and lower your legs slowly. Bring them up into a fully vertical position if possible and then lower them again slowly. This strengthens the legs and back and tones up the stomach muscles.

Back strengthening

Turn on your front and use the Cobra exercise, raising the head and legs slowly to strengthen the back. Do this with your hands under your forehead and elbows out to the side. Don't expect a great deal of movement to start with.

Exercising with a club
With your feet wide apart, hold a golf club behind your neck, horizontally along your shoulders. Feel that you keep the knees and feet still and try to turn through a full right angle, first to the right then to the left. This is the movement needed in golf, with a twisting in the hips and back as you move fully through the swing.

Wall twists
The simple exercise for loosening up the back is to stand about 2 feet from a wall, with your back to it. Hold your arms and hands out in front of you and then simply twist and turn to touch the wall behind you in one direction. Twist and turn to touch it in the other direction. Try to make the movement in the back and hips, feeling that the knees and lower legs stay fairly still.

183

Sit-ups
Lastly, try sit-ups. Trap your feet under the edge of a bed or get someone else to hold your feet still while you lie on your back. Pull yourself up with the back and stomach muscles until your hands come up to touch your thighs and knees. Then lower yourself slowly, repeating this progressively more as your strength improves.

REMEMBER
GOOD GOLF
REQUIRES
STRONG LEGS

MONITORING IMPROVEMENTS

To improve your golf, you need feedback from other people. You also need to get some knowledge of results in order to benefit from practice.

When experimenting with your golf swing, only change one variable at a time. If you try to change more than one, you will not know what is having the effect. Perhaps, for example, you think you are standing too far from the ball, which is causing problems, and you also feel the ball may be too far forward in your stance. Don't change both at once. Experiment first on the distance from the ball and secondly with the ball position.

Always try to practise by using a set schedule and give yourself a plan for your practice before you go out. Don't just hit balls aimlessly without having a set idea in mind.

If possible, keep results of what you achieve so that you can see where the problems lie and also assess your improvement.

On the course, monitor your progress on the scorecard – not just in terms of your actual score, but in terms of achievements in other areas. If you improve certain elements of your game, the score itself will improve. On your scorecard, mark off the various columns and use these to give yourself information.

Make one column the number of drives where you hit the fairway. Give yourself a tick if you hit the fairway and an "R" or "L" for right or left, depending on where you miss it. Use the second column to mark how many greens you hit from under, say, 200 yards. Again, give yourself a tick if you hit the green and, for an experienced player, mark whether the ball is short or past – using an "S" or "P" or a plus or minus.

For the really advanced player, mark down the number of yards you are short or past the flag. If, for example, you finish 5 yards past the flag, put "+5". If you finish 10 yards short, put "–10". In this way you begin to see whether your clubbing is accurate.

Golfers will often find that they finish short of the flag on at least 15 or 16 of the holes. They never attack the hole. It is only by keeping a record such as this and giving yourself feedback that you become aware of your own shortcomings.

Mark, too, whether the ball is right or left of the flag. Some players will continually miss on one side without really realizing it. If you miss the green, where have you missed it? Right or left? Short or long? Again, make a note.

In another column assess your chips, pitches and bunker shots. Give yourself a tick if you pass the flag and a cross if you are short. One of the most common problems with scoring is when you are always short of the flag with your approach shot. You may find yourself short at least 80 per cent of the time. Again you may not realize the deficiency unless you keep a record.

In another column on the card you can assess your putting. How many putts did you take and from how far? Is the long putt short or past? See whether there is any pattern to your game that can be bettered without actually improving technique.

One of the most common reasons for not scoring as well as you should is through poor clubbing. On the whole, golfers under-club. They either feel they can hit the ball farther than they can or do not judge distances properly.

Distance on a golf course is not always easy to judge. It can be foreshortened and there is often an optical illusion in judging distance, with the positioning and size of bunkers, trees and so on.

Many golf clubs now have yardage charts available in the Pro Shop which give diagrams of each hole and the distances. Experiment on your own course, firstly by pacing off the distances that you hit for each club (carry, but not including run) and then also pace off the course so that you know how far you hit the ball and can also select clubs as accurately as possible.

Professional golfers hardly ever play competitively without precise knowledge of distances. They carry notebooks and make copious notes in practice rounds for use in the tornament. An example of recording the distance might look as shown here:

Hole 5 pine tree R fg 115 cg 128 bg 141 + 25.

This, in shorthand terms, means the pine tree right to the front of the green is 150 yards, to the centre of the green 128 yards, to the back of the green 141 yards, with 25 yards over the back of the green before any trouble.

Using their own shorthand, professionals will make a note of some distances, preferably about 20 yards behind their likely driving position, from which they can measure distance into the green. Most use these distances down to about 50 yards from the flag. They will then add on, mentally, 10 yards if playing into a light breeze, 20 yards if into a strong wind, and perhaps 10 yards if going uphill and so on.

Analyse your distances for various clubs, starting from the 5 iron and hoping for a differential of 10 yards between clubs up and down. Check your 3 and 4 irons, in particular, to see whether you really do manage to get an extra 10 yards between each of them.

When you reach the stage of taking competitive golf seriously, you need to make copious notes of the course you are playing during practice rounds, particularly of distances and hazards. Jot these down in shorthand for each of the holes. When practising, also keep a record of where your shots go at each hole, whether left or right, long or short, and how many putts you need – and how long.

(185)

COURSE

HOLE	FAIRWAY	GREENS under 200	CHIPS and BUNKERS	PUTTS	
1	✓ R	✓ S	—	30'	2
2	✓ L	✓ SR	—	15'	2
3	X	X SR	✓	8'	1
4	✓	X SR	X	10'	2
5	✓	✓ P	—		
6	✓	X SL			
7	X				
8					
10					
11					
12					
13					

COURSE COMMENTS

HOLE	COMMENTS
1	Back Trap R Pg 105 cg 125 bg 145 +15
2	Birch R to trap R 190 Trap L Pg 165 cg 180 bg 195
3	FT Pg 170 cg 186 bg 202 OB+5
	Trap L Pg 138 2nd tier 152 bg 172 ↘ +5
4	Pine tree R fg 115 cg 128 bg 141 +125
	210 Birch L cg 148 Trap

REMEMBER
FEEDBACK
IMPROVES
LEARNING

WATCHING PROFESSIONALS

When you go to a professional tournament, spend some time on the practice ground watching the players. Try to stand directly behind them so that you are looking down the line of the shot.

If you can, watch someone your own height to see just how he or she stands. Look at how close most professional golfers stand to the ball, with the impression of standing up tall.

Look for the inside takeaway and attack on the ball, the clubhead striking the ball with a curved path.

You will notice that almost all good professionals have excellent balance. It is this that allows for the tremendous clubhead speed, combined with good timing, which they achieve.

You will also see that the professional is almost always meticulous about lining up, often on the practice ground setting a clubshaft along the feet to ensure the stance is always parallel to the proposed line of the shot.

From any other view, and generally with shots on the course, watch the player and *not* the ball. If you watch the ball, you miss seeing the impact and follow-through. Watch professionals watching other professionals and see how they study the player, not the ball. Observe the routine and try to learn a definite pattern.

If you watch one professional for several holes, you will see how mannerisms are adopted and the pre-shot routine repeated. Often the routine is exactly the same for the way the ball is set up, the club waggled, target looked up at and so on. Try, too, to pick up the general rhythm and timing of a good professional player.

See how professionals use yardage charts for clubbing and how they pace off distances. You will see most good players with notebooks giving a distance from a set point on the fairway, then walking back or forward from that set point to assess the precise distance to the shot. You will also see how they meticulously

toss grass into the air to assess any wind and then choose the club very carefully.

Notice, too, how professional golfers attack the hole. Most want to be past the flag with every single shot. Again, if you watch one player, see how often he or she passes the flag with shots to the green – far more often than amateurs.

When you watch the short game, notice the punching attack of approach pitches, the head staying still and the restricted finish, the weight always going through on the left foot. Again, watch the player rather than the ball, so that you see what happens through and beyond impact.

On the putting green, the main lesson is to see just how still good players keep

their heads. Watch, too, for the routine, whether the player has a practice swing and the meticulous way in which he sets up to the ball. Don't, however, copy the slowness of many professionals in lining up their putts.

When looking at chipping, the main lesson is to see how close players stand to the ball, in general with a very short shot, and with the wrists arched up rather than dropped. Watch how, with most short shots professionals play, the throughswing mirrors the backswing for length, but always with a feeling of slight acceleration through the ball.

Try to understand the logic behind choosing clubs around the green and the

Watch the player and not the ball; the best place is on the practice ground.

use of the putter for running shots, particularly from bare lies.

Look at recovery shots. You will often see the professional golfer recovering with a safer and less ambitious shot than the club golfer would ever try.

Good players are prepared to zig-zag and will not always aim straight for the flag. Try to assess the players' thinking in terms of percentage golf as well as individual shots.

REMEMBER
WATCH THE
PLAYER, NOT
THE BALL

MASTERS OF DESIGN

The game of golf is all about the courses on which it is played. Each has its own character and, with championship courses in particular, a character that changes through the day and from day to day with the uncertainties of the weather and climate.

Early courses were, in the main, built almost entirely using the existing contours of the land. Very often bunkers simply developed on seaside links as the wind blew. There was little large scale earth-moving and the merit of any course depended on the choice of land and the route for navigating the natural hazards.

Where hazards were constructed, they were often deep and sometimes hidden. They were usually to catch a slightly less than perfect shot, rather than to dictate a particular route from tee to green.

Several men have been influential in the design and development of today's championship courses. Such courses have, as a rule, been allowed to retain their traditional characters and have not been altered by club committees.

Old Tom Morris (1821–1908)

As with most professionals of the day, Old Tom was also a greenkeeper, first at Prestwick and then at St Andrews. Among the courses he designed were Lahinch in Ireland, Westward Ho! in Devon, Muirfield and Royal County Down – four of the most highly regarded courses in the British Isles. Some suggested he was a genius, others that his genius was in seeing the wisdom to leave natural beauty well alone.

Henry Colt (1869–1951)

An amateur golfer and the first secretary at Sunningdale, Henry Colt adapted the original plans for the Old Course there – one of the world's finest inland courses – and designed the New Course. He also designed the courses at St Georges Hill, Wentworth, Rye and Swinley Forest, the last of these apparently his own favourite. Started in 1908, Swinley was possibly the first course carved through a forest and

bears Colt's distinctive stamp of stressing accuracy and strategy for each hole, rather than length.

Herbert Fowler (1856–1941)

Another amateur golfer, Herbert Fowler was the inspiration behind Walton Heath Old and New Courses and the Berkshire Red and Blue. His philosophy was to tamper as little as possible with what nature had created.

Tom Simpson (1877–1964)

A designer of several magnificent courses on the continent of Europe, including Chantilly and Morfontaine, Simpson's writing on golf course architecture in 1930 demonstrate the changes, good and bad, that have taken place.

"Avoid artificial work as much as possible ... contours of the green should be such that a player can always get dead with his first putt ... greens should be neither square, rectangular nor oblong, but irregular ... nine out of 10 greens that are not flat slope uphill; that is a mistake. The best greens are those that slope downhill, as at St Andrews. Limit the number of bunkers around a green to three, make them small and to eat well into the green. Never raise tees except for visibility and never make them square or oblong. The straight-fronted line is a foolish and mischievous convention and has a prejudicial effect on the mind of the golfer! The point where the fairway unites with the putting green or rough should be so indefinite as to be practically invisible."

In 1931 Simpson's calculations for constructing a course amounted to a mere £16,220 – including £4,250 for the greens, £2,000 for the preparation of the fairways, £4,000 for hazards, £1,575 for seed, £850 for the water supply, £1,260 for the contractor, £970 for the architect and £240 for the foreman and under-foremen for 30 weeks' labour.

Sixty years later, the same estimates run from around £300,000 to perhaps £2 million for the standard type of course Simpson envisaged.

Alister Mackenzie (1870–1934)

Arguably the architect who did more than anyone for golf course design was Dr Alister Mackenzie, a medic from Scotland who trained under Harry Colt. Mackenzie followed his designs of Alwoodley and Moortown at Leeds with the West Course at Royal Melbourne, Cypress Point in California and the Augusta National – home of the US Masters.

In 1920, Mackenzie set out his theories in a book, *Golf Architecture*. One of the more poignant of these was that there should be no punishment of having to look for a lost ball!

In conjunction with the legendary Bobby Jones, Mackenzie constructed the magnificent Augusta National, setting new standards and ideals for inland courses in America, with greens and contours that contrasted sharply with the traditional designs of the British championship courses.

Donald Ross (1873–1948)

Originally from Dornoch in Scotland, Donald Ross became America's leading golf architect with, amongst others, the following championship courses: Brae Burn, Oakland Hills, Inverness, Scioto, Seminole and Pinehurst No 2.

Robert Trent Jones Snr (1906–   )

Although born in Lancashire Robert Trent Jones lived in the United States from the age of four, where he became the most famous golf course architect of post-war years. He studied at Cornell University in an assortment of subjects – agronomy, landscaping and engineering – to prepare for his chosen profession. He was himself a good amateur golfer, before giving up serious playing of the game through poor health.

His business, carried on by his two sons, has adapted many top-class courses, often lengthening them for modern golf, as well as creating new ones. The typical Trent Jones course is long – 7,000 yards from the tiger tees – with plenty of artistically shaped bunkers and large undulating greens. The fairways are often very narrow and severely dog-legged. A valuable feature was that such courses could be made punishing for the professional in a tournament yet playable and enjoyable for the club golfer from forward tees and with the easier pin positions.

Trent Jones's courses in Europe include Moor Allerton in Yorkshire, the New Course at Ballybunion (a real old-fashioned links), Sotogrande and Geneva. Worldwide, Trent Jones's masterpieces include Dorado Beach in Puerto Rico, Cotton Bay in the Bahamas and Karuizaura in Japan.

It is in America that Trent Jones's main courses abound – Peachtree in Atlanta, Spyglass Hill in California, The Dunes and Hazeltine, where Tony Jacklin won the US Open. Jacklin loved it. Dave Hill, the runner-up, described it as a cow pasture and was subsequently fined for expressing his opinion.

That sums up Trent Jones architecture. The professionals either love it or hate it. Certainly it would have distressed Tom Simpson, with his ideas of naturalness, downsloping greens, small strategic bunkers, and fairways blending inconspicuously with the rough.

"Pete" Dye (1935–   )

Paul Dye (always known as "Pete") is another American architect who has his own distinctive and often controversial ideas about course design. A top-class amateur, Dye was apparently inspired with the idea of natural golf on his first visit to Royal Dornoch.

His courses are, as a rule, breathtaking for their beauty, if not daunting to the players. Amongst his finest are Hadon Town (Hilton Head), Campo de Golf Cajuiles (Casa de Campo) in the Dominican Republic, the PGA Tournament players' course in Florida and his new PGA West in California. If you visit a Pete Dye course, take your camera, but think twice about taking your clubs unless you are a good player!

Royal St Georges (left), a famous links course on the bleakest corner of the Kent coast, has recently regained favour as a venue for the British Open, which Sandy Lyle won there in 1985.

Turnberry (below left), the venue for the British Open and popular with Americans. A typically rugged and often windswept Scottish course, containing the spectacular 9th hole, where you have to tee off high above the rock-smashing waves.

St Andrews (below), inspiration for many of the early golf architects, uses all the natural humps and hollows and has barely changed for almost 200 years. It is the golfer's dream to be walking up the famous 18th to the clubhouse on the way to the Open title.

191

CONNOISSEURS' FAVOURITE COURSES

Gleneagles (above) — a delightfully scenic inland Scottish course that provides one of Britain's most luxurious golfing resorts for those who can afford to stay and play there.

Augusta National (right) is home of the US Masters and the inspiration of Bobby Jones and Alister Mackenzie. Each spring top professionals and amateurs play for the coveted green jacket, which is awarded to the winner. Prize money matches the importance of the event but, by tradition, is rarely mentioned.

**Royal Melbourne
(right)** is Australia's
oldest golf club. The
West Course, designed
by Alister Mackenzie, is
generally regarded as one
of the world's finest
inland courses and a
frequent venue for the
Australian Championship.
With the East Course, it
is used as a venue for
both the World Cup and
World Amateur Team
Championship.

Sunningdale (below):
the Old Course, which
was designed originally
by Willie Park in 1900
and constructed and
maintained under the
supervision of Harry Colt,
is one of Britain's finest
inland courses. A firm
favourite of the true golf
connoisseurs, it is not
only scenic but requires
perfect placement of
every shot. Three short
par 4s — the 3rd, 9th and
11th — between 272 and
304 yards — prove the
point that length is not
everything.

193

THE WATERY GRAVES

Vale do Lobo (above) is one of the most popular courses on Portugal's Algarve. This view, from the 16th tee, highlights the attraction of the venue of the Portuguese Open.

Pebble Beach (right), is a US Open Championship course on the Californian coast where in 1984 Tom Watson held a superb chip on the 17th to snatch the title from Jack Nicklaus, the master himself.

The PGA West (left),
and the celebrated
17th hole on the Stadium
Course in California,
typify Pete Dye's design
at its best — or worst!
The course is a master of
golfers at its most
spectacular, or perhaps
its most ridiculous.
Playing a Pete Dye
course is a memorable
experience and makes
most other courses seem
dull by comparison.

195

Dhahran, Saudi Arabia (left and below left): here grass is at a premium, although that does not deter the golf enthusiast. Players have to take round their own mat or piece of Astroturf from which to play each shot.

197

St Pierre, Chepstow (below) is a classic British parkland course and frequent scene of major professional championships. This pretty Welsh venue has played host to the Curtis Cup between the ladies of Britain and America.

COURSES AROUND THE WORLD: 2

Crans-sur-Sierre (right), a mountainous and naturally spectacular course, one of the most scenic in Europe and venue for the Swiss Open.

At Akureyri (below right) golf is played in Iceland against magnificent backdrops. One great advantage in midsummer is that you can play 24 hours a day — provided you have the stamina.

Singapore (below) is the place to go for rich, lush fairways and greens. This beautifully manicured course plays host to one of the largest memberships in the world.

THE GREENKEEPER'S ARMOURY

When you step out on to a course to play a round, it is all too easy to take for granted the fact that all the tees, fairways and greens have been properly prepared – and, for that matter, hazards such as the bunkers.

This is all made possible by the greenkeeper and his team of workers, who daily tend the course – from brushing the early dew off the greens to cutting new holes, raking the bunkers or mowing the fairways.

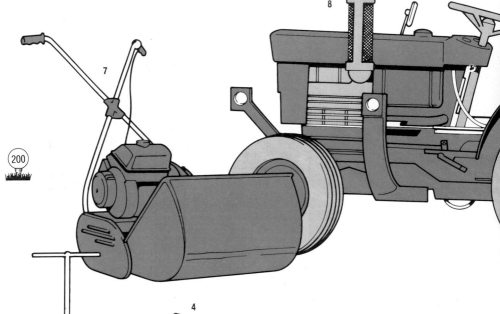

Here is a selection of typical equipment every greenkeeper needs to look after his course
7 Motor mower for fine turf cutting
8 An all-purpose tractor with the necessary attachments.
9 Aerator for spiking the grass
10 A gang mower attachment with three cutting units.
11 Turf cutter
12 Wide broom for brushing the greens

4 Hole-cutting board, used to prevent damaging the green around the new hole
5 Scissors to trim the grass around the edge of the hole
6 Tool for lifting the liner out of existing holes

The following items are for cutting new holes in the greens:
1 A hole-cutter
2 The hole liner
3 Mallet

RAKING THE BUNKERS

A special ride-on bunker rake, fitted with a rear-mounted, three-part rake and finisher, is designed to take out foot and club marks, leaving a perfectly smooth surface of sand in the bunkers. The wide tyres prevent the machine from digging into the sand.

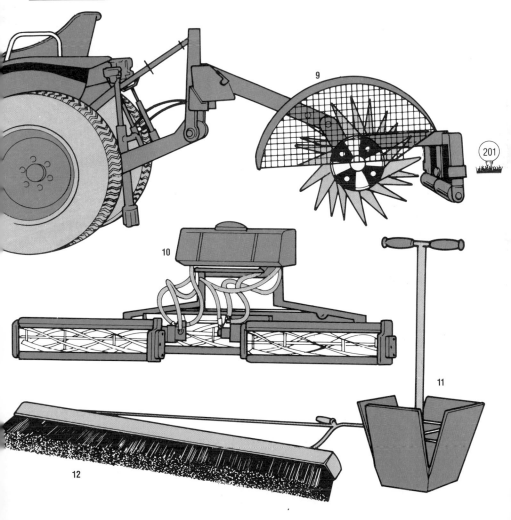

9

201

10

11

12

STROKEPLAY

Strokeplay – or medal play, as it is otherwise known – is generally considered to be the most testing form of competition, in which the total number of shots for the complete 18 holes is recorded. The scores for each hole are written down and added up to give the gross score.

The gross score is always used in professional competitions and championships. In amateur competitions, other than championships, the player's handicap is deducted to give the nett score. The lowest gross score wins the scratch prize and the lowest nett score the handicap prize.

In strokeplay, you are playing against a whole field of players rather than one specific opponent. For this reason, the rules and penalties for matchplay and strokeplay differ. In strokeplay your playing partner is correctly known as the marker. Before starting the round, players exchange scorecards and mark each others cards throughout.

The strokeplay format is the one used for assessing handicap. It can be played as a singles, foursomes or fourball.

Seve Ballesteros (right), one of the hardest competitors in the professional game – here very much at home during the 1987 Spanish Open.

Dos and don'ts of strokeplay

There is much to the tactical, thinking side when you are involved in strokeplay. When you first start this form of competition, you will not, of course, remember everything. But try and keep as much as possible in the back of your mind. It could make the difference between winning and losing.

● Don't become big-headed if things are going well.
● Don't think: "What if?" It signifies stress.
● Don't anticipate the score before the last shot is played.
● Do remember that a bad start does not mean a bad round.
● Put the score out of your mind until the match is over. If you are doing well, you may get over-excited; if doing badly, it can worry you and make things worse.
● Don't assume your final score will be double that of the first nine holes. A score can be made up of 45 out and 35 in or 35 out and 45 in. Keep going.
● Don't think about what you are going to win until you've won it.
● Don't worry about making the winner's speech until you know you've won the competition!

● The only form of forward thinking you should do is to plan each hole as you get to it.
● See where the flag is and plan your drive carefully.
● Don't plan ahead. You must think firmly in the present.
● Hit the shot and then forget it. Walk to the ball and just concentrate on the next shot, then the next ... and so on.
● Always play one shot at a time in your mind.
● Don't choose the club until you get to the shot or you will muddle your thinking.
● Think of each shot for itself. Don't remind yourself of shots past or anticipate shots to come.
● If you make a mistake, put it out of your mind as quickly as possible.
● Don't adjust your play for any hole because of the score. Use your normal approach to any one shot, regardless of where you stand in the match.
● Don't take unnecessary risks, particularly with recovery shots or those that contain elements of a gamble. If you feel things are going badly, you may make them worse.

MATCHPLAY

This is the form of competition in which you compete hole by hole against one individual or a partnership. It is different from strokeplay, in which you are competing against the whole field of players on the score. In matchplay, the player with the lower score on each hole wins that hole, playing either level or off handicap.

Assume, for example, that A is playing a match against B and they are playing level. A wins the first hole with a four to B's five. A goes one up and correctly B should stay at the score that he is – one down. On the second hole, both players have five and they therefore halve the hole and A remains one up. A wins the third and goes two up, while B then is two down.

Say A is eventually three up after 15 holes, that is three up with three to play. We now say that he is dormie three, meaning that he cannot lose unless they go into extra holes. A and B halve the 16th, so that A remains three up with only two holes left. At this point B cannot catch him and so we say that A has won by three holes up and two holes to play, abbreviated to 3 and 2.

If, for example, B won the 16th, 17th and 18th, the players would finish the match all square. It would depend on the rules of the competition and the format as to whether they went on to play extra holes. That would mean going down to the 1st again, which now becomes the 19th. Or the match ends there.

If it is a knockout competition, then they would go on to the 19th, 20th and so on until there was a definite winner. If it is a club or international match, then often the play would finish at the 18th and a halved match would be recorded.

Here are some points on etiquette:
● On the first tee you should toss for who gets the honour of playing first, unless there is a set draw saying who should play. It is not correct simply for the lower handicap to go first.
● The player who wins the hole gets the honour on the next tee and drives first. He keeps the honour until the other player wins a hole.
● Correctly the player who is *down* should declare the score after each hole. This is not always done, but it should be. There is no need to keep a card of the match, provided this is done. In matchplay, you do not hole out and the hole by hole score is not relevant.
● If receiving a stroke when playing matchplay under handicap, the player receiving the stroke should announce this. He is responsible for claiming the stroke.

Rules for matchplay and strokeplay differ. In matchplay you are playing only against your opponent, whereas in strokeplay you are playing against the whole field.

It is not possible to go back and change the score. You must also state correctly the number of shots taken, if asked. If you do not, and do not correct the information before your opponent plays, you forfeit that hole. This is an example of a rule that does not apply in strokeplay.

The thinking side

This is very important in matchplay. As a general rule, try to play matchplay in the same way as strokeplay; in other words, just play the course and try to build up a good score without thinking too much about what your opponent is doing. If your opponent plays a bad shot, do not alter the way you play the next one.

Don't change your approach to a hole until you know what your opponent has scored. It is very easy to assume he is going to hole a putt of, perhaps, 4 feet. If you are too bold with your 10-footer and he then misses his, you will probably miss yours as well.

Remember that the match is not lost or won until the final putt is holed, and to think positively about the shot in hand, as you would in strokeplay. If you were five up and are now only two up, forget what is past.

Sandy Lyle driving for victory at the 14th in the 1988 Suntory against Nick Faldo.

204

CARDS AND HANDICAPS

In golf it is vital to understand the relevant terminology, particularly in relation to par and handicap.

First, take a player who is a good amateur of international standard. We will call him the scratch player. Par, or the standard scratch, is the measure of how he should play around a golf course.

On a hole of up to 250 yards (220 yards or so for the ladies), we assume that the scratch player will hit the green in one shot and will take two putts. So we call this hole a par three. A par four, then, is anything from 251 yards to approximately 470 yards, where we assume the scratch player will take two shots to get to the green, plus two putts, giving a par four.

A par five is from approximately 471 yards and longer, where we assume our scratch player will take three to reach the green, plus two putts again, making a par five. Adding the pars for each of the 18 holes gives the total par for the course. In most situations this is the same as what is called the standard scratch. In the case of the card shown here, the standard scratch score (SSS) is 70.

This total varies slightly from one country to another and for ladies golf, of course. But it is this total – the SSS – from which handicaps are assessed.

The scratch player, who hopes to go round in a score equal to the SSS, will be a player of amateur international or club professional standard.

A four handicap player would hope to go round in four shots more than the standard scratch, making him a player of roughly club first team standard. The maximum handicap for men is generally 28 and, in theory, anyone on that handicap should go round the course in 28 shots above the standard scratch. But anyone with a higher score than this will still be given a 28 handicap.

For the ladies, the maximum handicap is usually 36, meaning that a player would hope to go round in 36 shots above the standard scratch.

206

Date	COMPETITION ABBOTSLEY OPEN			Tee	Handicap	Strokes Rec
Player A	VIVIEN SAUNDERS				SCR	
Player B	JULIAN WORTHINGTON				15	15

Markers Score	Hole	White Yds.	Yellow Yds.	Par	Index	Strokes Received A / B	Gross Score	Result or Points A / B	LADIES TEES Yards	Par	Index		
	1. Corncracker	337	331	4	13			4 5	321	4	15		
	2. Windy Ridge	367	360	4	9			4 4	353	4	7		
	3. Park Way	410	385	4	3			5 4	393	4	5		
	4. The Stumps	311	300	4	11			4 6	303	4	11		
	5. Saxons Hamlet	341	332	4	17			3 5	306	4	9		
	6. Mousehole	133	121	3	15			3 4	97	3	17	3	14
	7. Abbotsley Rise	298	284	4	7			4 5	269	4	13	4	8
	8. Downs	455	446	4	1			4 5	400	5	1	5	2
	9. Briar Hill	370	356	4	5			4 4	340	4	5	3	16
	OUT	3022	2915	35				35 42	2782	37		4	10
												5	4
	16. Barley Slice	450	382	4	2			4 5	397	5	6		
	17. Barford View	241	234	3	12			4 3	235	4	18		
	18. Final Fling	406	299	4	10			4 4	290	4	12		
	IN	3128	2865	35				36 37	2750	37			
	OUT	3022	2915	35				35 42	2782	37			
	TOTAL	6150	5780	70				71 79	5532	74			
	HANDICAP							- 15					
	NETT							71 64					

S.S.S. WHITE 71 YELLOW 68 RED 72

PAR WHITE 70 YELLOW 70 RED 74

Markers Signature .... Players Signature V. Saunders

Filling in a scorecard for a strokeplay competition. Each player fills in a card recording both players' scores at each hole. Depending on your handicap, you should deduct that from your total gross score at the end of the round. This represents the number of strokes received. As a scratch player you would not receive any strokes.

Looking at the scorecard, you will see there are various columns. First is the column marked "Yardage", which shows the distance of each hole, measured from a set point on the teeing ground to the centre of the green via the middle of the fairway.

The next column shows the par of that hole. For men, this usually depends solely on distance and for the ladies on a combination of distance and difficulty.

The column marked "Stroke Index" is used in handicap competitions and is followed by the columns for completing the score. On the back of the card you will usually find the local rules and a column showing how to calculate handicaps for different competitions.

The column marked "Stroke Index" is used when golfers play a match against each other, and also in some forms of competition, explained later, such as the Stableford Bogey or Bogey Competition. In a handicap match between, for example, a nine handicap and a 21

handicap, there is a handicap difference of 12. In a singles match you would take threequarters of this difference, giving a difference of nine.

Looking at this card, the 21 handicap will receive a stroke from the lower handicap on each of those holes in the stroke index column which has the number nine or less against it. He receives nine shots in total from these holes, deducting one from each of his scores before matching it against his opponents. If the match were halved and the players went down to the 19th, he would start taking strokes again on the same stroke index holes.

On the back of the card are details of the local rules. A common one allows players to pick stones out of the bunkers and gives precise definitions of any out of bounds round the course.

The scorecard often has details of the handicap calculation used for foursome and singles matches and in the forms of Stablefords and Bogey competitions.

In a Stableford, you are awarded points per hole based on the net number of strokes taken. The way to fill in the scorecard is as shown here. In this case, player A receives 13 strokes and should therefore tick each hole that has an index of 1 to 13. This means he receives a stroke at each of these holes. On the basis that you receive 3 points for a birdie, 2 points for a par and 1 point for one over par, put down the number of points scored at each hole, depending on your net number of strokes, and total all 18.

Date	COMPETITION ABBOTSLEY STABLEFORD					Tee	Handicap	Strokes Rec
Player A	JULIAN WORTHINGTON						15	13
Player B	VIVIEN SAUNDERS						SCR	—

Markers Score	Hole	White Yds.	Yellow Yds.	Par	Index	Strokes Received A	B	Gross Score A	B	Result or Points	LADIES TEES Yards	Par	Index
4	1. Corncracker	337	331	4	13	✓		5		2	321	4	15
4	2. Windy Ridge	367	360	4	9	✓		5		2	353	4	7
4	3. Park Way	410	385	4	3	✓		4		3	393	5	3
4	4. The Stumps	311	300	4	11	✓		5		2	303	4	11
5	5. Saxons Hamlet	341	332	4	17	–		4		2	306	4	9
3	6. Mousehole	133	121	3	15	–		2		3	97	3	17
4	7. Abbotsley Rise	298	284	4	7	✓		6		1	269	4	13
5	8. Downs	455	446	4	1	✓		6		1	400	5	1
4	9. Briar Hill	370	356	4	5	✓		5		2	340	4	5
37	OUT	3022	2915	35						18	2782	37	

												3	14
												4	8
												5	2
												3	16
												4	10
												5	4
4	16. Barley Slice	450	382	4	2	✓		4		3	397	5	6
3	17. Darford View	241	234	3	12	✓		5		1	235	4	18
4	18. Final Fling	406	299	4	10	✓		5		2	290	4	12
36	IN	3128	2865	35						14	2750	37	
	OUT	3022	2915	35						18	2782	37	
	TOTAL	6150	5780	70						32	5532	74	
	HANDICAP												
	NETT												

S.S.S. WHITE 71 YELLOW 68 RED 72   PAR WHITE 70 YELLOW 70 RED 74

Markers Signature V.Saunders   Players Signature

COMPETITIONS

Handicapping makes it possible for players of unequal skill to compete on level terms. This allows a variety of match formats so that there's always a contest that's fair for the players and conditions on a given day.

There are competitions for six or more players in a group – useful on a day when the course is congested; and others which encourage speedy play or spare the diffident beginner the anguish of teeing off in front of the crowd at the first hole.

The standard games are described here. They can be the basis of more complex arrangements to suit the occasion.

Strokeplay
This is the form of competition in which the player totals his score for each of the 18 holes, giving a gross score before deduction of handicap and a nett score after deduction of handicap. The full handicap is deducted from the gross score to give the nett score. This is usually considered the most testing form of golf.

Matchplay
This is the head-to-head match between two players. If played off handicap, the lower handicap player gives threequarters of the handicap difference to the higher handicap player, the strokes being taken by following the stroke index column on the scorecard.

Foursomes
In this, four golfers play together in pairs, but use one ball between a pair and take alternate shots for each hole. One player elects to drive the first hole and will then drive on every odd numbered hole; the other takes the even ones. This can then be played on a matchplay or strokeplay format. In America this is usually referred to as "Scottish Foursomes".

Four Ball Better Ball
This is a form of play in which four players play together, each using a ball. It is played in partnerships, matching the lower score of each of the partnerships in a matchplay format. Four Ball Better Ball can also be played in strokeplay form. In a match, the handicapping is taken on a threequarter basis, the players taking handicap strokes from the lowest handicap of the four.

Greensomes
In this competition, players go out in fours, made up of two pairs. All four players drive on each hole. The players of each partnership choose the better drive of the two and finish the hole playing alternate shots. The player whose drive was not taken plays the second shot. Some clubs use a handicap system for this, just taking the average of the two handicaps. Others use what is generally a fairer system, taking six-tenths of the lower handicap plus four-tenths of the higher handicap. A Greensome can then be played as a match, a medal or a Stableford Bogey.

The Stableford or Stableford Bogey
This is a popular form of competition against par (derived from the old name for par of "bogey"). In this, the player takes seven-eighths of his handicap against par, according to the stroke index. In other words, a 24 handicap would receive 21 strokes and gets one stroke on each hole plus a stroke on those in the index marked one, two or three.

On the card, he fills in the gross score and then, after mentally deducting the strokes, counts two points for a hole completed in par or nett par, one point for a score or nett score of one over par, three points for a birdie or nett birdie, four for an eagle or nett eagle, and so on. The player with the most points for the 18 holes wins, with the winning scores usually ranging from 35 to 42 points.

The Stableford form of competition can be played in singles, foursomes, four ball or greensomes.

Bogey Competition
This is an alternative to the Stableford Bogey and is, in effect, a matchplay

competition in which the golfer plays a hole-by-hole match against par (bogey). The player receives threequarters of his handicap and takes those in the form of strokes from par according to the stroke index.

Unlike a true match, the whole round is completed and the player records on each hole whether, after receipt of his strokes, he has won or lost the hole against bogey. At the end of the round he records how many up or down he is against par, for example three up or six down. This is a difficult form of competition with winning scores anything from two up to two down.

Bisque Bogey

In a match or bogey competition, an adaptation is to use "bisques". These are, in effect, strokes that can be taken where a player chooses, instead of at an allotted hole. In a Bisque Bogey the player would, for example, receive perhaps 15 strokes and can elect, after playing the hole, whether or not to take one of his bisques. In a similar way, a match can be played in which one player gives another six bisques and he can decide when he wants to take them.

Eclectic Competition

This is a type of competition run, as a rule, over a period of weeks or months, in which the player records his best score for every hole taken over that same period. There are various ways of playing an Eclectic Competition. In some cases, players are allowed unlimited cards and in others they are restricted. As a general principle, after completing the initial round, the player tries to improve the score for each individual hole before the usual deduction of half handicap.

Flag Competition

Here the player is allotted a certain number of strokes to use for the round, being the par of the course plus his handicap. In other words, a 20 handicap golfer playing on a par 70 course is given 90 strokes to use. He starts off from the first tee and, after playing 90 strokes, places a small flag with his name on where the 90th shot finishes. The person who finishes nearest the 18th hole or farthest up the first or second fairway for the second time round is the winner.

St Andrews Greensome

The St Andrews Greensome is similar to an ordinary Greensome, except that the players alternate in taking the second shots. In other words, one player elects to take the second shot on the odd numbered holes and the other on the even ones. They still both drive and elect the better drive for the next player to play.

Texas Scramble

This is a team competition, usually four-up. Each player drives off the first tee. The team captain then chooses the best drive and all the players take their ball to this position. They all then hit a shot from there. The captain again chooses the best second shot. Everyone else takes their ball to that spot and continues until the first player has holed out.

Build up to strokeplay

Even the less experienced golfers want to go for strokeplay because that is what the professionals play. But it is the hardest form of competition. You should start with Stablefords and Bogeys, in which you do not always have to putt out. If you start off with medal competitions and get heavily beaten, you can soon become demoralized. And remember – always balance competition with practice.

ETIQUETTE

Etiquette is very important on the golf course, so much so that it forms the first section of the Official Rules of Golf published by the Royal and Ancient Golf Club of St Andrews and the United States Golf Association. It is part of the tradition of golf, but is also important for safety.

Learn about golfing etiquette as soon as possible, so that even if you are a high handicap golfer, you will always be welcome on a golf course.

Here are some key points that are basically just good manners:

● Don't walk or move while others are playing.
● Always try to be aware of others playing behind you and let them through if you are holding them up. Remember that a player may hit the ball 250 yards and may be waiting for you, even though he seems a long way away. If you are losing ground on the match in front, be prepared to stand aside and wave other players on. Once you have waved them on, let them go. Particularly if you lose a ball, be quick in waving other players through. And if you do find your ball, don't then try and get back in front of them again.
● Always be punctual on the first tee and never have practice swings on a tee.
● Replace divots and repair pitch marks on the greens.
● If you go into a bunker, always enter it from the back and never down the face unless your ball is right in the face. Rake the bunker well to smooth over your footprints. If there is no rake, use your clubhead.
● On the green, don't walk on the line of another player's shot. Always step carefully across it if you are going up to attend the flag. And when attending the flag, first see that it is loose and will pull out of the hole easily. Secondly, stand away from the hole to the side and don't cast your shadow over the hole. Thirdly, hold the flag to keep it from flapping in the wind. Finally, pull it out immediately the player has struck his putt.

● State the score in a match at the end of every hole if you are the player who is down. If you are the one who is up, state the score if your opponent fails to do so.
● When marking your ball on the green, use a small coin or ball marker and place it behind the ball before picking it up. When replacing it, put the ball down in exactly the spot it came from and then pick up the marker. If, for some reason, you have to ask a player to mark his ball to the side, then remind him to replace it in the right spot.

Etiquette is also vital for safety
● Always stand to the right of the shot and never behind a player.
● On the tee, always go over to the right side of the tee to watch another player. This is crucial for safety. Remember that on a tee the other person may hit his drive, not be satisfied with it and then take a practice swing while you are possibly walking forward to take up your position.
● Never get ahead of a player, and never turn your back on someone who is playing, however expert. Always keep level with him and on the correct side.
● If there is any likelihood of your ball hitting someone else, or if it is going over trees toward an adjacent fairway, call out "fore". If you hear someone else shout "fore", don't just look around to see whether they mean you, but bend over and cover your head with your arms.
● Always wait until the players in front are out of range. When hitting to the green, wait until they have cleared it and are well to the side before you play on.
● Finally, try to play golf at a reasonable speed. When you get to the tee, don't mark your card for the previous hole, if you are the first player to drive. Get on the tee as quickly as possible, but take time over your shot. Other players should then get their drivers out and be ready, again marking the card if necessary while going up to the next fairway. Don't mark your card on the green or even by the green after finishing the hole.

Procedure on the green is one part of the etiquette of the game that you need to be well aware of. This includes the correct way of attending the flag. The best way of learning this routine is to watch the professional caddie during a tournament. The main points to remember are to stand clear of the hole to prevent casting a shadow over it and not to let the flag flap in the wind. Both can be very distracting when your opponent is trying to putt.

211

● Get used to leaving your clubs on the correct side of the green as near as possible to the exit to the next tee.
● Move quickly between shots so that other players are not delayed.
● If you think you have lost a ball, get used to using the provisional ball rule. This will avoid the bother of having to go back to the tee.

● The rules state that you are allowed five minutes to look for your ball. If you think that it could be lost, check your watch immediately you arrive on the scene, be prepared to call other players through from behind you, and only use that five minutes. In a four ball, assume that each player is responsible for his own ball and keep play moving.

POINTS FROM THE RULES

The ball should be played as it lies, which means that you cannot improve its lie except on the tee. Here you can tread down behind it or pick pieces of grass from behind the ball, but you cannot do this anywhere else on the course.

If you lose a ball, play another one from the spot where the original one was hit and add a shot. This is known as stroke and distance. In other words, if you lose a ball with your drive, the next one will be three off the tee.

If you think you have lost a ball, you can play a provisional ball up to the spot where you think the original one was lost. State that you are playing a provisional ball. If the first ball is lost, you can go on with the provisional one. If the first ball is found, then the provisional one must be abandoned and you should go on with the first one or declare it unplayable.

If the ball is unplayable (through the green), which means anywhere other than hazards or the tee or the green of the hole being played, then you have three choices. The first is to take your ball out two club-lengths from its position no nearer the hole and add a penalty of one stroke. Secondly you can take stroke and distance and go back to the spot from where the original came. Thirdly you can go back as far as you like, keeping the spot where the unplayable ball was between yourself and the flag.

In a bunker, you have the same options if the ball is unplayable. But if you are picking up two club-lengths or going back as far as you want, this must still be in the bunker. The only way you can pick out of a bunker is by taking stroke and distance, in other words going back to where the original shot came from.

Identify your ball
Be careful to play the correct ball. Remember its make and number and, in competitions, put an identifying mark on it. If you play the wrong ball in strokeplay, you will be penalized two strokes for each shot you play with that wrong ball to a maximum of four strokes.

If you play the wrong ball in matchplay, you lose a hole. If you play the wrong ball in a bunker, there is no penalty providing you then identify it as being wrong and do not play any more shots with that ball outside the bunker. You can then go back and find the right ball.

If you move a ball accidentally, penalties apply in both matchplay and strokeplay, other than on the green, where you replace the ball without penalty.

The rules of golf are quite complex. For example, take the difference between an outside agency and a rub of the green. Assume that a dog picks up a stationary ball and runs off with it. You would replace it with no penalty. If a dog picks up a moving ball and runs off with it, unless you are on the green this is known as a rub of the green and you simply play it from where the dog takes it. If it is lost altogether, then it must count as a lost ball. If, on the other hand, you have hit a ball with your putter on the green and a dog picks it up while it is moving, there is no penalty and you can replace and re-play it.

Wary of the wet
Basically, casual water and ground under repair should not be on the course. You therefore have a free drop within a club-length of the nearest point of relief. If you are on the green and water lies between you and the flag, you can move around to the side to take relief. But if you are chipping to the flag and the water is in the way, you cannot get relief.

In the way
Obstructions can be either movable or immovable. What is movable to one person may become immovable to another. If movable, for example the greenkeeper's rake or a drinks can, then you can move it and there is no penalty if you should inadvertently move the ball. Movable obstructions are man-made items and do not include natural objects such as tree branches or twigs. If obstructions are immovable, then you must move the ball

by finding the nearest point of relief, no nearer the hole.

Over the water

There are two sorts of water hazard – standard and lateral. With a standard water hazard, you must cross it at some point. If your ball goes into it, you must take a penalty and can drop back as far as you like. But you must play your ball over the hazard.

A lateral water hazard runs down the side of a hole. If you go in the water, you can pick the ball out again for a penalty on either side of the hazard, level with the point where the ball crossed the edge of the water.

Teeing tips

Take care about playing from the wrong tee. Again there is a penalty in both matchplay and strokeplay. If you play in the wrong order in a match, in other words taking the honour off the tee when your opponent should, or if you tee up from outside the tee, your opponent has the option of recalling your shot. In strokeplay the latter would be a penalty.

It will pay dividends to learn all the differences between matchplay and strokeplay.

Obstructions

A loose impediment is a natural object such as a leaf or twig, whereas a movable obstruction is something like a piece of paper, a cigarette end or a greenkeeper's rake.

In a bunker you cannot move any natural object unless the local rule says to the contrary and allows you to remove stones. You can, however, remove movable obstructions, in other words man-made items, without penalty and would incur no penalty if your ball were moved in doing so.

Governors of the game

Golf's rule book contains only 34 entries. But "clubs" take a page and a half to describe and the specifications for the ball detail the tests that are applied (at 23 deg. C) to establish its legality, including maximum velocity off the tee.

The game has had formal rules since 1774. Since the 1890s, most of the world has acknowledged the Royal and Ancient Golf Club of St Andrews as the final authority; in recent years the Rules of Golf Committee, which invites representatives of the world's leading golfing nations to join it, has worked with the United States Golf Association, the only other governing authority, so that there are now world-wide standards.

A Decisions Sub-Committee answers queries. If they lead to interesting interpretations, loose-leaf revisions for the Rules of Golf are circulated around the world. A present concern, dealt with by another committee, is that new materials and technology used in the making of clubs and balls shall not give players unfair advantage or, indeed, defeat the object of established golf course design.

One rule change, in 1952, succeeded in removing the primary meaning of a colloquial word from the English language. A "stymie" was the situation when an opponent's ball was on the putting surface between another player's ball and the hole. It could not be moved. Now it can – and the word stymie passed out of golf but endures in the language to describe other frustrations.

213

GOLFING TERMS

Words indicated in SMALL CAPITALS are included as individual entries.

Address the golfer's position when preparing to hit the ball.

Airshot swinging at the ball and missing completely.

Albatross a hole completed in three shots less than par; also known as a "double eagle".

All square in MATCHPLAY, when players are even in the match.

Approach shot one whose target is the green.

Approach putt a putt not aimed directly at the hole but "laying up" close enough to make the next putt a certainty.

Backspin the spin on the ball applied by the loft on the clubface. A skilled player may apply extra backspin to stop the ball rolling forward on landing.

Backswing the first part of the swing, when the club is taken away from the ball to behind the shoulder.

Better ball when the lower score in a partnership is recorded for each hole.

Birdie a hole that is completed in one under par.

Bisque in a match played to handicap, a stroke which can be claimed where the competitor chooses, rather than at allotted

SCORE INDEX holes. It is taken after the hole is played.

Blaster alternative name for the most lofted club, the sand wedge.

Bogey a hole completed in one over par; formerly, in Britain, an alternative name for par.

Bogey competition the player receives three quarters of handicap and records performance against par, e.g. 2 up (on par), 3 down (on par).

Borrow the slope of the green's surface; in response, the player "borrows" to the left or right.

Bunker a depression in the ground, usually, but not always, filled with sand, designed to catch mishit balls. In the US, also known as a "trap" or "sand trap".

Bye unofficial match played over the rest of the course when a MATCHPLAY competition has been won before the 18th hole has been played.

Caddie a helper who carries a player's bag around the course and may advise on the course or the game.

Carry the distance a struck ball travels through the air.

Casual water water on the course which is not part of the design, such as rain puddles or over-irrigated areas. If a ball is in such water or, to play it, the player's feet would be, one can take a free DROP. If there is casual water on the green, a ball on the green may be moved to the nearest place equally distant from the hole from which a putt will avoid water.

Centre-shaft style of putter in which the shaft attaches to the middle of the head.

Chip a short running shot with a medium iron from just off the edge of the green.

Closed a relationship between the direction of the stance and the clubface. The clubface is "closed" or "shut" if it is angled toward the feet; the stance is "closed" if the front foot is across the target line.

Cup the tubular lining sunk in the hole. Also, the hole itself.

Dead a ball so close to the hole that it can be assumed the next putt is unmissable; in MATCHPLAY that putt is conceded.

Divot the sliver of turf cut *after* the ball is struck by a well-hit iron shot.

Dormie in MATCHPLAY, when a competitor leads by as many holes as there are left to play.

Downswing the part of the golf swing from the top of the backswing to striking the ball.

Draw a shot with a slight, controlled curve through the air, from right to left (right-handed player).

Driver the 1 wood, the most powerful club in the set, used for getting maximum length off the tee.

Drop when a ball must be lifted, under penalty or otherwise, the player, standing erect, holds the ball at arm's length and shoulder height and drops it not nearer the hole.

Eagle a hole completed in two under par.

Eclectic a competition over several weeks or months, in which players record their best scores on every hole of the course.

Explosion shot the shot at a ball embedded in the sand of a bunker.

Face the surface of the clubhead that strikes the ball.

Face insert the extra hard impact area set into the face of a wooden club.

Fade a shot designed to curve slightly in the air, from left to right (right-handed player).

Fairway the cut grass, and proper route, between tee and green.

Fairway woods 2, 3, 4, 5 and sometimes higher-numbered woods designed to be used when the ball is in play after the tee shot.

Flag the marker that shows the position of the hole on the green.

Flag competition each competitor plays the number of shots derived from adding par for the course to their handicap. The player who gets the farthest (marking the place with a flag) is the winner.

Flange the broad sole of an iron club, particularly exaggerated on a sand wedge.

Flat swing one in which the club's motion around the body is low.

215

Follow-through the part of the swing beyond impact with the ball.

"Fore" the shouted word by which golfers warn others on the course that they are in danger of being hit by a ball.

Fourball match between four players, usually two a side, using a ball each. The better score of each team at each hole counts.

Foursome match between two pairs of players, each side playing one ball and taking alternate shots. Tee shots are taken alternately.

Fringe the collar of slightly longer grass around the close-mown putting surface of the green.

Grain the angle at which the grass of a green grows. Putting "against the grain" requires more effort than "with the grain".

Green the closely mown, carefully manicured target area in which the hole is cut.

Greensomes type of match for two pairs of players. All four drive at each hole and finish it playing alternate shots off the better drive. The handicap used by each side is six-tenths of the lower handicap and four-tenths of the higher.

Grip the position of the hands on the club; also, the leather binding or rubber sleeve by which the clubshaft is held.

Gross score the number of shots taken to complete the course, before deduction of handicap to give the nett score.

Ground under repair area of a course temporarily out of play, from which a ball

may be removed for a DROP without penalty; a ball outside the area may also be moved if the lie would cause the player to stand in it.

Half when opponents register the same score. A match is "halved" if it is completed all square.

Handicap rating of a player's skill relative to par for the course. A 20-handicap player should complete a par 70 course in a score of 90. This stroke allowance permits players of unequal skill to compete on terms.

Hanging lie when the ball is on ground sloping down ahead of the player.

Hazard any permanent obstacle on a course, such as a bunker or ditch.

Heel the part of the clubhead beneath the end of the shaft.

Hole the hole, $4\frac{1}{4}$ inches in diameter, into which the ball is played.

Honour to play first off the tee, the privilege of the winner of the preceding hole.

Hooded when the clubface is turned CLOSED and inward, reducing its loft.

Hook faulty stroke when the ball curves to the left (right-handed player).

Hosel the extension to the clubhead into which the shaft fits.

Lateral water hazard a ditch, stream or pond roughly parallel to the line of the hole. A ball picked out may be played from either side, with a one stroke penalty.

Lie the position in which the ball comes to rest; also, the angle between the clubhead and shaft which may vary to suit short and tall players.

Links a seaside golf course, typified by sand, turf and coarse grass, of the kind where golf was originally played.

Local rules clarification of points about unusual features or obstacles on a course, itemized on the back of the scorecard.

Loft the angle on the clubhead to produce more or less height; also, to make the ball rise.

Long game the shots in which achieving distance is important.

Loose impediments twigs and leaves, not actually growing, and not adhering to the ball, which may be removed from around it without penalty. The ball must not be moved.

Lost ball if after five minutes searching a ball cannot be found, a competitor is penalized one stroke and plays another ball from the spot where the first one was hit, counting as the third shot.

Mark to idenfity the spot on the green where a player has picked up a ball for cleaning or to clear the way for another player's putt.

Marker the player who keeps a record of another's score.

Matchplay contest decided by the number of holes won rather than the total number of shots.

Medal play strokeplay; contest decided by the lowest number of shots.

Nett score a player's score for a round after the handicap allowance has been deducted.

Open of the clubhead, when it is turned out at the toe; of the stance, when the line of the feet is to the left of the target (right-handed player).

Out of bounds ground officially outside the playing area, marked by lines of posts or fences. A ball hit into it must be replayed from the original spot, and a penalty stroke is added.

Par the number of shots a scratch player is expected to take on a hole or a course.

Penalty in strokeplay, a rule infringement usually costs two strokes; in matchplay, the hole is generally lost.

Pin informal name for the flagstick in the hole.

Pitch shot a short shot to the green, hit high so that it will not roll on landing.

Provisional a ball played when it seems likely that the preceding shot is lost or out of bounds. It will count, plus a penalty stroke and the first stroke, if the original ball is not found; if it is, the provisional cannot be used.

Pull a straight shot to the left of the target (right-handed player).

Push a straight shot to the right of the target (right-handed player).

Putt the rolling shot taken on the green, with a putter.

Rough the area of less kempt grass and vegetation bordering the fairway.

Rub of the green when a ball is stopped or deflected accidentally. It has to be played where it lies.

Rules the world of golf is administered by the Royal and Ancient Golf Club of St Andrews (the R and A) and the United States Golf Association (USGA). Local rules may be set by a club to cope with peculiarities on its course.

Sand trap in the US, a bunker.

Sand wedge iron, the most lofted club in the set, for playing bunker shots and pitches.

Scratch player one who is expected to play the course in par.

Set of clubs the maximum allowed is 14, usually 4 woods, 9 irons 1 putter.

Shank area of an iron's clubhead at the HOSEL; hence a shot hit by the clubface at this point, which flies off to the right (right-handed player).

Short game approach shots to the green, and putting.

Shut see CLOSED.

Single one player against another.

Slice faulty shot which curves left to right in the air (right-handed player).

Sole the underside of the clubhead.

Square the position of the body at the ADDRESS when it is parallel to the line of the ball to the target.

Stableford a form of competition against par, using $\frac{7}{8}$ of handicap according to the stroke index. Nett par scores 2 points; one over, 1 point; a birdie, 3 points.

Stance the player's position when the feet are set, in alignment, ready to play the ball.

Standard Scratch Score the assessment of par for a course and the basis for handicapping.

Stroke a shot in golf.

Stroke and distance the penalty of one stroke and the return to the site of the shot before, when a ball is lost, out of bounds or otherwise unplayable.

Stroke index the numbers on a scorecard indicating the order of the holes at which a handicap player receives strokes.

Strokeplay competition decided by the number of shots taken.

Swingweight measure of balance and overall weight of clubs; in a match set, all club should feel the same when swung.

Tee, teeing ground flat, sometimes raised, area from which first shots at each hole are played. There may be several: men's competition tee ("the tiger tee"), men's tee, forward men's tee and ladies' tee.

Texas scramble team competition in which all players play from the site of their team's best drive, best second shot, and so on.

Three off the tee if a ball is lost, out of bounds or unplayable from the tee shot, the player is penalized one stroke and tees off again – the third shot.

Threesome a match in which one player competes against two, each side playing one ball.

Throughswing the part of the swing during which the ball is actually hit.

Through the green the golf course, apart from teeing grounds, putting greens, hazards and out of bounds areas.

Toe the area of the clubhead farthest from the shaft.

Top to hit the ball above its centre; a topped shot does not rise off the ground.

Trap in the US, a bunker.

Unplayable a player may choose to deem a ball unplayable, taking a penalty stroke and DROPPING the ball no nearer the hole. A ball that is unplayable in a bunker must be dropped in the bunker or STROKE AND DISTANCE taken.

Uphill lie when the ball is positioned on ground sloping up ahead of the player.

Upright swing style in which the clubhead movement is almost vertical.

Waggle a player's loosening-up movements at address.

Wedge a club with an extremely lofted face: pitching and sand irons.

Whipping the closely bound binding at the head of a wooden club.

Wrist cock the natural hingeing of the wrist which begins as the club is lifted on the backswing.

Naming the clubs

In the days when golf was played with a feathery, a leather cover filled with feathers, the clubs had names rather than numbers. These are the best known:

Baffie any wooden face with a lofted face for fairway use.

Brassie 2 wood.

Cleek driving iron, a 1 iron.

Mashie 5 or 6 iron.

Niblick 7 or 8 iron.

Spoon fairway wood, particularly a 3 wood.

INDEX

Main entries are indicated in bold numerals.

ACKNOWLEDGEMENTS

Picture credits, photographs

l = left; *r* = right; *t* = top; *c* = centre; *b* = bottom;
fl = far left; *fr* = far right

3, 7 & 9 Peter Dazeley; 10 E T Archive; 11
Lawrence N Levy/Yours in Sport; 12*t* & *b* St
Andrews University Photographic Collection; 13
Lawrence N Levy/Yours in Sport; 14 St Andrews
University Photographic Collection; 15*t* Hulton
Deutsch Collection; 15*b* Associated
Newspapers/Popperfoto; 17 Yours in Sport; 18
David Cannon/Allsport; 19*t* Leo Mason/Split
Second; 19*b* David Cannon/Allsport; 20*t* David
Cannon/Allsport; 20*b* Mark Newcombe Photography;
21*t* David Cannon/Allsport; 21*b* Mike King/Split
Second; 22*t* & *b* David Cannon/Allsport; 23 *tl*
Popperfoto; 23*tr* Peter Dazeley; 23*b* Allsport; 26/7 &
28*t* St Andrews University Photographic Collection;
28*b*, 29 *fl*, *l* & *r* Dunlop Slazenger International; 29
fr Peter Dazeley; 83 Lawrence N Levy/Yours in
Sport; 138 Mike King/Split Second; 139 Stewart
Kendall/Sportsphoto Agency; 152/3 Steve
Moore/*Today's Golfer*; 155 Lawrence N Levy/Yours
in Sport; 186/7 Charles Briscoe-Knight; 190 Leo
Mason/Split Second; 190/1 David Cannon/Allsport;
191 Mark Newcombe Photography; 192*t* Aspect
Picture Library; 192*b* Peter Dazeley; 193*t* Sporting
Pictures; 193*b* David Cannon/Allsport; 194 Mark
Newcombe Photography; 194/5 J Alex
Langley/Aspect Picture Library; 195 David/Allsport;
196 Anthony Howarth/Susan Griggs Agency; 196/7
David Higgs/Aspect Picture Library; 197/8, 198/9
Phil Sheldon; 199 Peter Dazeley; 203, 205 & 211
Lawrence N Levy/Yours in Sport.

Additional line illustrations
29, 42/3, 44/5 Jerry Gower; 38–41, 176–183 Coral
Mula; 200/1 Simon Roulstone; 185 Jonathan Bigg

Index by Donald Binney

Special thanks to Bill Hughes, Cambridgeshire Golf
Centre Huntingdon, 69a High Street, Huntingdon,
Cambs.